Legal Pr
of
International Banking

AUSTRALIA AND NEW ZEALAND
The Law Book Company Ltd.
Sydney : Melbourne : Perth

CANADA AND U.S.A.
The Carswell Company Ltd.
Agincourt, Ontario

INDIA
N. M. Tripathi Private Ltd.
Bombay
and
Eastern Law House Private Ltd.
Calcutta and Delhi
M.P.P. House
Bangalore

ISRAEL
Steimatzky's Agency Ltd.
Jerusalem : Tel Aviv : Haifa

MALAYSIA : SINGAPORE : BRUNEI
Malayan Law Journal (Pte.) Ltd.
Singapore and Kuala Lumpur

PAKISTAN
Pakistan Law House
Karachi

Legal Problems
of
International Banking

By

F. R. Ryder, LL.B., F.I.B.
of Gray's Inn, Barrister.

London
Sweet & Maxwell
1987

Published in 1987 by
Sweet & Maxwell Limited
of 11 New Fetter Lane, London.
Computerset by Promenade Graphics Limited, Cheltenham
Printed in Great Britain by
Page Brothers (Norwich) Ltd.

British Library Cataloguing in Publication Data

Ryder, F. R.
    Legal problems of international banking.
    1. Banks and banking, International—
    Law and legislation
    I. Title
    342 6'8215 K1066

ISBN 0-421-36780-6

All rights reserved.
No part of this publication may be
reproduced or transmitted, in any form
or by any means, electronic, mechanical, photocopying,
recording or otherwise, or stored in any retrieval
system of any nature without the written permission
of the copyright holder and the publisher, application
for which shall be made to the publisher.

©
SWEET & MAXWELL
1987

Preface

This volume updates the substance of the Gilbart Lectures of 1971, thought to be the first publication ever specifically tackling legal problems associated with commercial international banking. Since that time books have been published dealing with the legal aspects of longer-term finance in which banks participate reflecting the utilisation of their large capital bases. At the same time the Institute of Bankers have introduced into their syllabus a new subject "Law and Practice of International Banking." However, as with the original lectures, the primary purpose of this book is as a handbook for bankers and lawyers alike so that they can find preliminary guidance and warning regarding traditional foreign banking business in which legal problems arise.

F. R. Ryder
1987

Contents

Preface	v
Table of Cases	ix
Table of Statutes	xv

I Introduction: The Law in the Background	1
Bankers and the Law	1
The Resolution of Problems	3
The Sources of the Solution	3
Jurisdiction	3
Conflict of law	5
Characterisation	6
II The Primary Banking Functions	7
The Practical Problems	7
The paying banker	8
The collecting banker	11
The type of customer	13
The Lending Banker	18
Securities	20
Conclusion	22
III Insolvency and the Secondary Functions	23
Insolvency	23
Insolvent companies	25
The Banker Creditor	27
Inactive Companies	29
Priorities	30
Guarantees and Indemnities on Behalf of Customers	33
The counter indemnity	34
The type of guarantee	35
The essential features	36
When claims are made	37
Summary	38
Documentary credits	38
The indemnity	38

The meaning of the indemnity	39
Another possibility	39
The Banker as Bailee and Agent	41
Secrecy	43
IV Government Intervention	45
Expropriation	45
The effects	46
Recognition of a foreign government	46
The law in England	47
The bankers problems	49
Summary	52
Currency Problems	52
How a currency obligation may be satisfied	53
The consequences for the banker	54
Exchange controls	55
Summary	57
Euro-dollars	58
The substance of the agreement	59
The law governing the contract	59
Availability	61
Summary	62
Conclusion	62
Appendix A	63
Appendix B	64
Index	65

Table of Cases

Anderson [1911] 1 K.B. 896 31
Anderson v. Equitable Life Assurance Society (1926) 134 L.T.
  557; [1926] All E.R. Rep. 93; 42 T.L.R. 302, C.A. 53
A/S Tallina Laevauhisus v. Estonian State S.S. Line (1947) 80
  Ll.L.Rep. 99, C.A. 48
Azoff-Don Commercial Bank [1954] Ch. 315; [1954] 2 W.L.R.
  654; 98 S.J. 252; [1954] 1 All E.R. 947 .... 27, 29

Banco de Bilbao v. Sancha [1938] 2 K.B. 176; [1938] 2 All E.R.
  253; 107 L.J.K.B. 681; 159 L.J. 369; 54 T.L.R.R. 603; 82
  Sol.Jo. 254, C.A. 51
Bank voor Handel em Scheepvart v. Slatford [1953] 1 Q.B. 248;
  [1951] 2 T.L.R. 755; 95 S.J. 546; [1951] 2 All E.R. 779; 31
  A.T.C. 535 49
Banque Belge pour L'Etranger v. Hambrouck [1921] 1 K.B.
  321; 90 L.J.K.B. 322; 37 T.L.R. 76; 65 Sol.Jo. 74; 26
  Com.Cas. 72, C.A. 51
Barclays Bank Ltd. v. Astly International Trust [1970] 2 Q.B.
  527; [1970] 2 W.L.R. 876; [1970] 1 All E.R. 719 11
Berliner Industriebank A.G. v. Jost [1971] 2 Q.B. 463; [1971] 3
  W.L.R. 61; 115 S.J. 505; [1971] 2 All E.R. 1513, C.A.;
  affirming [1971] 1 Q.B. 278; [1970] 3 W.L.R. 743; 114 S.J.
  492; [1971] 2 All E.R. 117 25
Bowling v. Cox [1926] A.C. 751; 95 L.J.P.C. 160; 135 L.T. 644,
  P.C. 43
Brimnes, The; Tenax Steamship Co. v. Brimnes, The (Owners)
  [1975] Q.B. 929; [1974] 3 W.L.R. 613; 118 S.J. 808; *sub
  nom.* Brimnes, The; Tenax Steamship Co. v. Owners of the
  Motor Vessel Brimnes [1974] 3 All E.R. 88; *sub nom.*
  Tenax Steamship Co. v. Brimnes, The (Owners); Brimnes
  The [1974] 2 Lloyd's Rep. 241, C.A.; affirming *sub nom.*
  Tenax Steamship Co. v. Reinante Transoceanica Nave-
  gacion S.A.; Brimnes, The [1973] 1 W.L.R. 386; 117 S.J.
  244 9
British and French Trust Corporation v. New Brunswick
  Railway [1939] A.C. 1; [1938] 4 All E.R. 747; 108
  L.J.K.B. 115; 160 L.T. 137; 55 T.L.R. 260; 83 Sol.Jo. 132;
  44 Com.Cas. 82, H.L. 53

British Imex Industries Ltd. v. Midland Bank Ltd. [1958] 1
    Q.B. 542; [1958] 2 W.L.R. 103; 102 S.J. 69; [1958] 1 All
    E.R. 264; [1957] 2 Lloyd's Rep. 591 38

Calico Printers Ass. v. Barclays Bank Ltd. (1931) 145 L.T. 51;
    36 Com.Cas. 197, C.A. 12
Charron v. Montreal Trust Co. (1959) 15 D.L.R. 240 14
Choice Investments Ltd. v. Jeromniman and Midland Bank
    Ltd. [1981] Q.B. 149; [1980] 2 W.L.R. 80; (1980) 124 S.J.
    883; [1981] 1 All E.R. 225, C.A. 14
Cocherall v. Dickens (1840) 3 Moo.P.C. 98; 2 Moo.Ind.App.
    353; 1 Mont.D. & De G. 45; 13 E.R. 45, P.C. 31
Commercial Bank of S. Australia (1886) 33 Ch.D. 174; 55
    L.J.Ch. 670; 55 L.T. 609; 2 T.L.R. 714 27

De Beeche v. South American Stores Ltd. [1935] A.C. 148; 104
    L.J.K.B. 101; 152 L.T. 309; 51 T.L.R. 189; 40 Com.Cas.
    157, H.L. 86
De Nichols v. Curlier [1900] A.C. 21; 69 L.J.Ch. 109; 81 L.T.
    733; 48 W.R. 269; 16 T.L.R. 101, H.L.; reversing S.C. *sub
    nom.* Re De Nicols; De Nicols v. Curlier [1898] 2 Ch. 60,
    C.A. 18
Didisheim v. London Westminster Bank [1900] 2 Ch. 15; 69
    L.J.Ch. 443; 82 L.T. 738; 48 W.R. 501; 16 T.L.R. 311,
    C.A. 18

Ellis v. McHenry (1871) L.R. 6 C.P. 228; 40 L.J.C.P. 109; 23
    L.T. 61; 19 W.R. 503 32
Esal (Commodities) v. Oriental Credit [1985] 2 Lloyd's Rep.
    546, C.A. 34

Feist v. Société Intercommunicale Belge de l'Electricité [1934]
    A.C. 161; [1933] All E.R. Rep. 228; 103 L.J.Ch. 41; 50
    T.L.R. 143; 78 Sol.Jo. 64; 39 Com.Cas. 145; 150 L.J. 41,
    H.L. 53

Galbraith v. Grimshaw [1910] A.C. 508; 79 L.J.K.B. 1011; 103
    L.J. 294; 54 Sol.Jo. 634; 17 Mans. 183, H.L. 28, 31
Gibbs v. Société Industrielle des Métaux (1890) 25 Q.B.D. 399 .. 32
Goater (1874) 30 L.T. 620; 22 W.R. 935, L.JJ. 24

Halesowen Presswork & Assemblies v. Westminster Bank. *See*
    National Westminster Bank v. Halesowen Presswork &
    Assemblies.

Imperial Loan Co. v. Stone [1982] 1 Q.B. 599; 61 L.J.Q.B. 449;
    66 L.J. 556; 56 J.P. 436; 8 T.L.R. 408, C.A. 17

Joseph & Richard Ltd. *v.* Lindley (1905) 3 C.L.R. 280 12

Kahler *v.* Midland Bank Ltd. (1950) A.C. 24; 66 T.J.R. (Pt. 1) 441; 94 S.J. 208; [1950] 1 All E.R. 405; 43 R. & I.T. 180 56
Keene *v.* Midland Bank Ltd. [1967] Ch. 182; [1966] 3 W.L.R. 779; 110 S.J. 847; [1966] 3 All E.R. 631; [1966] 2 Lloyd's Rep. 475 11
Kleinwort Sons & Co. *v.* Ungarische Baumwolle Industrie Akt. & Hungarian General Credit Bank All E.R. 38; (1939) 2 K.B. 678; 108 L.J.K.B. 861; 160 L.T. 615; 55 T.L.R. 814; 83 Sol.Jo. 473; 44 Com.Cas. 324, C.A. 56

Levasseur *v.* Mason & Barry Ltd. (1891) 2 Q.B. 73; 60 L.J.Q.R. 659; 64 L.T. 761; 39 W.R. 596; 7 T.L.R. 436, C.A. 32
Lloyds Bank *v.* Savory (EB) & Co. [1944] A.C. 201; 102 L.J.K.B. 224; 49 T.L.R. 116; 38 Com.Cas. 115 1
Lorentzen *v.* Lydden Co. Ltd. [1942] 2 K.B. 202; 111 L.J.K.B. 327; 167 L.T. 363; 58 T.L.R. 178 49
Luther, A. M. *v.* Sagar, J. & Co. [1921] 3 K.B. 532 48

Macaulay *v.* Guaranty Trust Co. of New York (1927) 44 T.L.R. 99 30
Mackesy *v.* Ramesays, Bonas & Co. (1843) 8 E.R. 628; (1843) 9 Cl. & Fin. 818 12
Mansouri *v.* Singh (1984) 134 New L.J. 991 56
Mareva Companies Naviera SA *v.* International Bulk Carriers SA [1975] 2 Lloyd's Rep. 509; (1975) 119 S.J. 660 64
Marfani & Co. *v.* Midland Bank [1968] 1 W.L.R. 956; 112 S.J. 396; [1968] 2 All E.R. 573; [1968] 1 Lloyd's Rep. 411, C.A.; affirming [1968] 1 W.L.R. 956; [1967] 3 All E.R. 967 1
Marrache *v.* Ashton [1943] A.C. 311; [1943] All E.R. 276; 112 L.J.P.C. 13; 59 T.L.R. 142; 87 Sol.Jo. 174, P.C. 34
Miliangos *v.* George Frank (Textiles) Ltd. [1976] A.C. 443; [1977] Q.B. 489; [1976] 3 W.L.R. 477; 120 S.J. 450; [1976] 3 All E.R. 599; [1976] 2 Lloyd's Rep. 434 53
Multiservice Book-binding Ltd. *v.* Marden [1979] Ch. 84; [1978] 2 W.L.R. 535; (1977) 122 S.J. 210; [1978] 2 All E.R. 489; (1977) 35 P. & C.R. 201 53

National Bank of Greece and Athens S.A. *v.* Metliss (1958) A.C. 509; [1957] 3 W.L.R. 1056; 101 S.J. 972; [1957] 3 All E.R. 608, H.L.; affirming *sub nom.* Metliss *v.* National Bank of Greece and Athens S.A.; [1957] 2 Q.B. 33; [1957] 2 W.L.R. 570; 101 S.J. 301; [1957] 2 All E.R. 1, C.A. 61

National Westminster Bank v. Halesowen Presswork & Assemblies [1971] 1 Q.B. 1; [1970] 3 W.L.R. 625; [1970] 3 All E.R. 473, C.A.; reversed [1972] A.C. 785; [1972] 2 W.L.R. 455; 116 S.J. 138; [1972] 1 All E.R. 641; [1972] 1 Lloyd's Rep. 101, H.L. 35
Novello & Co. v. Hinrichsen Edition Ltd. [1951] Ch. 595; [1951] Ch. 1026; [1951] 2 T.L.R. 645; [1951] 2 All E.R. 451; 68 R.P.C. 243 48

Pelegrin v. Coutts & Co. [1915] 1 Ch. 696; 84 L.J.Ch. 576; 113 L.J. 140 18
Princess Olga Paly v. Weisz [1929] 1 K.B. 718; 98 L.J.K.B. 465; 141 L.T. 207; 45 T.L.R. 365; 73 Sol.Jo. 283, C.A. 48
Pyrmont Ltd. v. Scholt [1939] A.C. 145; [1938] 4 All E.R. 713; 108 L.J.P.C. 30; 160 L.T. 118; 55 T.L.R. 178; 83 Sol.Jo. 133, P.C. 54

R. v. Lovitt [1912] A.C. 212; 81 L.J.P.C. 140; 150 L.J. 650; 28 T.L.R. 41, P.C. 23
Rekstin v. Severo [1933] 1 K.B. 47; 102 L.J.K.B. 16; 147 L.T. 231; 48 T.L.R. 578; 78 Sol.Jo. 494, C.A. 9
Robinson ex p. (1883) 22 Ch. D. 816; 48 L.T. 501; 31 W.R. 553, C.A. 31
Russian Commercial and Industrial Bank v. Comptoir d'Escompte de Mulhouse [1925] A.C. 112; 2 K.B. 630; 92 L.J.K.B. 1053; 129 L.J. 706; 39 T.L.R. 561; 68 Sol.Jo. 2, C.A. 29

Scottish Life Assurance Co. v. John Donald [1901] S.L.T. 200 22
Selangor United Rubber Estates v. Cradock (No. 3) [1968] 1 W.L.R. 1555; 112 S.J. 744; [1968] 2 All E.R. 1073; [1968] 2 Lloyd's Rep. 289 17
Seldt's Trusts (1902) 1 Ch. 488; 71 L.J.Ch. 192; 46 Sol. Jo. 280 ... 14
Sharif v. Azad [1967] 1 Q.B. 605; [1966] 3 W.L.R. 1285; 110 S.J. 791; [1966] 3 All E.R. 785; [1966] C.L.Y. 10471, C.A. 57
Siskina, The [1979] A.C. 210; [1977] 3 W.L.R. 818, 121 S.J. 744; [1977] 3 All E.R. 803; [1978] 1 C.M.L.R. 190; *sub nom.* Siskina (Owners of Cargo Lately on Board) v. Distos Compania Naviera [1977] 3 All E.R. 803; (1977) 121 S.J. 744; (1978) 1 Lloyd's Rep. 1, H.L.; reversing [1977] 2 Lloyd's Rep. 230; (1977) 121 S.J. 461 64
Société des Hôtel Le Touquet v. Cummings [1922] 1 K.B. 451; 91 L.J.K.B. 288; 126 L.T. 513; 38 T.L.R. 221; 66 Sol.Jo. 269, C.A. 53
Solomons v. Ross (1764) 1 Hy.Bl. 131; 126 E.R. 79 .... 28, 31
Soproma S.p.A. v. Marine and Animal By-products Corporation (1966) 1 Lloyd's Rep. 367; 116 New L.J. 867 40

South India Shipping Corp. *v.* Export-Import Bank of Korea
[1985] 1 W.L.R. 585; (1985) 129 S.J. 268; [1985] 2 All
E.R. 219; 1985 P.C.C. 125; [1985] 1 Lloyd's Rep. 413;
[1985] F.L.R. 106; [1985] 82 L.S.Gaz. 1005, C.A. reversing 16
Stern *v.* R. [1896] 1 Q.B. 211; 65 L.J.Q.B. 240; 73 L.T. 752; 44
W.R. 302 21
Swiss Bank Corporation *v.* Bohemische Bank [1923] 1 K.B. 673;
92 L.J.K.B. 600; 128 L.T. 809; 39 T.L.R. 179; 67 Sol.Jo.
423, C.A. 10

Theophile *v.* The Solicitor General [1950] A.C. 186; 66 T.L.R.
(Pt. 1) 441; 94 S.J. 208; [1950] 1 All E.R. 405; 43 R. & I.T.
180; affirming *sub nom. Re* A Debtor (No. 335 of 1947), *ex p.*
R. *v.* The Debtor, 64 T.L.R. 446 24
Treseder-Griffin *v.* Co-operative Insurance Society Ltd. [1956]
2 Q.B. 127; [1956] 2 W.L.R. 866; 100 S.J. 283; [1956] 2 All
E.R. 33; [1956] 1 Lloyd's Rep. 377, C.A.; reversing [1955]
3 W.L.R. 996; 99 S.J. 912; [1955] 3 All E.R. 793; [1955] 2
Lloyd's Rep. 527 53

Urquart *Re* (1890) 24 Q.B.P. 723; 59 L.J.Q.B. 364; 38 W.R.
612; 7 Morr. 94, C.A. 24

Vide, Haile Selassie *v.* Cable and Wireless (No. 2) [1939] Ch.
182; 108 L.J.Ch. 190; 160 L.T. 120; 55 T.L.R. 209 50

Wagg, Helbert [1956] Ch. 323; [1956] 2 W.L.R. 183; 100 S.J.
53; [1956] 1 All E.R. 129 60
Williams and Humbert *v.* W. & H. Trade Marks (Jersey)
(1986) 83 L.G.Gaz. 37; (1986) 136 New L.J. 15, H.L.;
Ramasa S.A. *v.* Multinvest (U.K.) affirming [1985] 3
W.L.R. 501; [1985] 2 All E.R. 619, C.A.; affirming (1985)
129 S.J. 573; [1985] 2 All E.R. 208 45
Winans *v.* Attorney General [1910] A.C. 27; 79 L.J.K.B. 156;
101 L.J. 754; 26 T.L.R. 133; 54 Sol.Jo. 133, H.L. [1908] 1
K.B. 1022, C.A. 21
Woodhouse A.C. Israel Cocoa S.A. *v.* Nigerian Produce
Marketing Co. [1972] A.C. 741; [1972] 2 W.L.R. 1090;
116 S.J. 329; [1972] 2 All E.R. 271; [1972] 1 Lloyd's Rep.
439, H.L.; affirming [1971] Q.B. 23; [1971] 2 W.L.R. 272;
[1971] 1 All E.R. 665 55

Z *v.* A-Z and AA-LL [1982] 2 W.L.R. 288; (1982) 126 S.J. 100;
[1982] 1 All E.R. 556; [1982] Q.B. 558; [1982] 1 Lloyd's
Rep. 240, C.A. 64

Table of Statutes

1882	Bankruptcy Act (4 & 5 Geo. 5, c. 59)—		1952	Income Tax Act (15 & 16 Geo. 6 and 1 Eliz. 2, c. 10)—
	s. 1 (*a*)	24		s. 468 (7) 25
	(*b*)	24	1972	European Communities Act (c. 68)—
	(*c*)	24		
	(*d*)	24		
	s. 22	28		s. 1 15
	s. 121	28	1985	Companies Act (c. 6)—
	Bill of Exchange Act (45 & 46 Vict. c. 61)—			s. 409 16
				s. 462 21
				s. 665 .... 26, 29
	s. 72	8		s. 666 26
				(5) 26
				s. 691 26

Publication of this book coincided with the bringing into force of the Insolvency Act 1985 by its consolidation with the Insolvency Act 1986 at the end of December 1986. It repealed the Bankruptcy Act 1914 (except sections 121 to 123), the Law of Property Act 1925, s.172, and the Companies Act 1985, ss.615 and 616; this occurred at different dates for different provisions. No attempt is made in the book to indicate the impact in the international field at the various dates when the new law was brought into force, which is the policy also of other similar concurrent publications.

I

Introduction: The Law in the Background

BANKERS AND THE LAW

Whether banking is regarded as a profession or a business, at present the emphasis is on the latter, it has much in common with other activities by which a community survives. It results from the division of labour and is subject, therefore, to the unending forces of specialisation, so long as there is a demand for what it has to offer. Among those engaged in its continuance there has grown up a fund of knowledge and a wealth of practice just as in any other pursuit. The practice, the routine, enables banking to function. The absence of specific thought as to "what" and "why" in everyday instances is essential to operations involving the quantity expected in specialised production. Yet the business is carried on within the framework of the law. The rights and liabilities of all concerned are, in theory, pre-ordained. The system works because, both explicitly and implicitly, the custom of the trade, the usage and, in more modern times, the practice, is allowed to "bend" the law. (In a less unhappy connotation the law recognises a "course of dealing" not only among individuals but among groups of individuals engaged in the same business.) Bankers have only to note the number of cases in recent years where either the existence of a practice has won the day, or, alternatively, in which the judge has deplored the absence of evidence of banking practice.[1] Admittedly there are exceptions. For example negligence in the collection of a cheque may often be disproved by evidence of what other bankers do or would have done. Of course if the habit is, of its nature, clearly negligent—it is not for example, a matter of degree, such as the size of the cheque or the seriousness of the enquiry involved—then the law will prevail.[2]

It follows that the reason a banker needs to know something of the law is to assess the risk he is taking. Needless to say, this comment has no reference to the criminal as distinct from the civil law. The question is as to the consequences in terms of money if there is a

---

[1] *Marfani* v. *Midland Bank Ltd.* [1968] 1 W.L.R. 956.
[2] *Lloyds Bank* v. *Savory (E.B.) & Co.* [1944] A.C. 201 where the practice of ignoring enquiries, that would otherwise have been made, solely because a cheque was paid in at another branch, failed to help the bank.

default, a broken promise, or a dispute, or, sometimes, on a controversial point, if the law eventuates to be other than what it was thought to be. The banker will want to know this. Often he will have to measure it against other considerations, the value to him of his connection, the goodwill that he may create and, again, particularly today, the profitability of the transaction. When he has decided what to do he will look to his legal adviser to suggest the ways in which the risks may be minimised. Traditionally bankers, and in fact most of the City of London, have sought to protect themselves from insolvency rather than from fraud, regarding the latter as inherently excluded by their own judgment and their customer's reputation. Nevertheless, with the broadening of the basis of commercial activity in the community, the possibility of the less venial defection, has increased in the last decade.

For the international banker all that has been said is applicable, but in a different degree. Division of labour and specialisation have greater play because of the greater variety and complexity of business. Practice exists internationally but has less influence on legal consequences because the law and the courts of different countries are involved. It is true that in relation to the more commonplace transactions, trading, bills of exchange and documentary credits, as well as promissory notes, the practice has often become the law, either by reason of generations of communal conduct or by ad hoc conventions such as that obtaining at present in relation to documentary credits.[3] In international business the risk is greater and the profit is expected to be commensurate. Yet there are other compensating factors.

The institutions involved are on an average larger and, therefore, prima facie more creditworthy than those concerned in domestic business. In banking, in particular, many international transactions are arranged through other bankers. They are often the buffers insulating the commercial parties from each other's frailties. The measure of confidence and the acceptance of the word among some international bankers is as unquestioning as between first-class domestic institutions. Admittedly these relationships are subject to the quirks, vicissitudes and quarrels of the respective Governments, but often businessmen, with their last contacts before a war and their first contacts afterwards, are a source of easing tension.

Just as the domestic banker will wish to know the law to assess the risk, so does the international banker. His risks are greater. His lawyer is less able to be precise because, as we shall see, the contingent factors are more numerous. Yet, business thrives. Internationally the trader is so often protected by dealing through bankers. Bankers internationally know each other more closely than do the customers and have immense confidence in one another's integrity. Their staff

---

[3] The Uniform Customs and Practice for Documentary Credits 1984.

are normally specialised, often doing automatically from experience in a crisis what their lawyers would advise after much consideration. In fact, in some Continental banks, quite a number of managers are lawyers and have transferred to and from the bank's legal department. Internationally, more than domestically, it is appreciated that law is business. Slowly the negative aspect of the mere need to satisfy the lawyer as a hurdle to be overcome, rather than to obtain suggestions from him in the early days of a project, is disappearing.

So we have the need of the international banker to know the law, a more complex matter than for a domestic banker, but, again, his concern is the risk. He expects his legal advisers not only to sound a warning but to provide solutions. These may be achieved in individual cases, or more generally by the establishment of codes of practice or conventions. It is in the milieu of international banking confidence that international trade progresses.

THE RESOLUTION OF PROBLEMS

As with all business the direct contact face to face with banking officials abroad facilitates the reduction of controversy. Probably the consequential reduction in a number of solicitor (or lawyer) drafted letters in itself eliminates a source of friction. So often a when lawyer drafts a letter he adverts to the likelihood of its being read by a judge. In international legal business, not the least in banking, because of the costs and the complexity the parties are more willing to take a view than in domestic legal disputes.

THE SOURCES OF THE SOLUTION

In relation to all international commercial legal problems there are three sources of solutions: jurisdiction, conflict of laws and characterisation.

Jurisdiction

Remembering always that it is is these practical consequences that are dominant here is one overriding legal aspect to examine. That is the subject of jurisdiction. Where an action may be brought and, above all, where a judgment may be pursued are essential questions. As is known from domestic banking, it is of little avail merely to win a law case. If the defendant has no assets or, to extend the principle to international banking, if the defendant has no assets in the country where the judgment can be enforced you may have only a pyrrhic victory. On the other hand the international banker probably cannot afford to have a judgment outstanding against him anywhere. If he does not have direct interest in assets in the particular country he will have an indirect interest in what might be attached, such as being a pledgee of his customer's goods. In conjunction it has to be recognised that the high standard of judicial administration of the Anglo-Saxon and continental countries (also, incidentally, of "arbitrations" in Moscow) does not obtain the world over. The late Professor E.J. Cohn has reminded us of this realistically in the following hypothesis[4]:

> "A small provincial town forming the centre of a perhaps still under-developed district, may be the seat of a court possessing jurisdiction to decide upon the most vital commercial dispute. Can one really expect a judge born, bred and residing in such a small town to be entirely impartial in a dispute in which the decision may result in taking the bread out of the mouths of hundreds of his fellow townsmen."

Similar fears of Machiavellian factors must obviously arise in some areas if the local Government, or even an arm of that Government, is a party to litigation or even indirectly interested in the consequences of a dispute. Thus, the vulnerability to proceedings in a foreign court is sometimes made more serious because of the unpredictable, or more cynically perhaps the only too predictable, outcome of the litigation. Again the delays and re-trials, permitted upon the most flimsy of pretexts, will occasionally result in frustration amounting to defeat.

The whole question of jurisdiction in relation to EEC countries, both as to the hearing of cases and as to the enforcement of judgments, has been revolutionised by the accession of the United Kingdom to the Brussels Convention of 1968 and its counterpart the Civil Jurisdiction and Judgments Act 1982 which was necessary for the provisions to have binding effect in the United Kingdom.

Some years ago it was recognised that the parties to a contract could provide that any disputes were by agreement to be subject to the courts of a particular country. In fact on June 22, 1977 the British Bankers Association published a reminder that an arrangement with a customer resident abroad could be made subject to the English courts by including an appropriate clause in a contract or mandate opening the account. The submission to the jurisdiction of an English court may come about in several ways. In particular it is to be noted that this may be achieved by written incorporation of a clear provision to that effect in the contract between the parties. Complementarily it is to be observed that where a clause between parties amounts to a submission to the jurisdiction of foreign courts, the courts in the United Kingdom will stay proceedings. Submission to a foreign court may be implied, as may be the case if a person domiciled in England is a member of a foreign company. In *Copin* v. *Adamson* (1874) L.R. 9 Ex. 345 a provision in the constitution (statutes)

---

[4] *Vide* International and Comparative Law Quarterly January 1965 in the course of an article in "*The Rules of Arbitration of the International Chamber of Commerce.*"

of a French company was regarded as an implied submission to the jurisdiction of the French Courts with the result that a stay of parallel proceedings in the United Kingdom was granted.

It will be seen that jurisdiction has two very important sides: first, that a judgment obtained in a foreign court may be enforced in the United Kingdom and secondly a judgment obtained in the United Kingdom will be enforced abroad. Statutes dealing with reciprocal enforcement *other* that in the EEC include the Reciprocal Enforcement Act 1933 and the Administration of Justice Act 1920. Similar and more effective legislation operates in relation to EEC countries.

Throughout this book we shall realise that the reciprocal enforcement is an aspect that bankers must always have in mind irrespective of the place concerned, not forgetting that in relation to the EEC countries the mechanism operates more effectively; this is because the mechanism authorisd by the other statutes is more cumbersome. Whilst it is acknowledged that a willingness to accept enforcement of the decisions of foreign courts in one's own country may be made conditional upon the preservation of overriding principles such as notification of the relevant proceedings and other aspects of what may loosely be thought of as natural justice, jurisdiction is a facet of the exercise of unrestricted power by Governments over things and people within their territory, varied by the extent to which they are willing to reduce that power by undertaking to accept and enforce decisions of courts in other countries.

Conflict of law

Another name for this subject is Private International Law, in distinction from Public International Law the principles of which govern the relationships between states in so far as Governments feel it wise politically, or socially, or economically to recognise them as binding. Conflict of laws is concerned with the extent to which any legal case involving a foreign element shall be decided wholly or in part according to English law or to the law of one or more of the foreign countries concerned. It might be asked why English courts should apply foreign law. There are a number of answers: first, there is the benefit of reciprocity; secondly, there is the intrinsic merit of achieving what the parties intended; thirdly, the result is likely to be far more just.

Whilst each country has its own principles there are certain common factors as one would expect; problems in relation to land are usually governed by the law of the country in which the land or building is situate. In the Latin countries nationality is accepted as determining a man's legal capacity whereas in Anglo Saxon countries the concept of domicile, equivalent to his permanent home, usually determines the capacity.

In one particular aspect there is a consequential problem; by

"Renvoi" is meant the application of the law of a foreign country in the sense that it is the decision that the courts of that country would in fact make and which may result from the application of the law of a third country. An example of a strange result of conflict of laws is in the case of *Embiricos* v. *Anglo Austrian Bank* [1905] 1 K.B. 677. A cheque on a London bank had been drawn in Rumania in favour of the plaintiff, who had endorsed it in favour of a London firm and put it in an envelope for posting to London. One of the clerks stole the cheque and forged the endorsement of the London firm and persuaded a Vienna bank, which acted in good faith and without negligence, to cash it for him. It was then sent to London, presented and paid. The payee, Embiricos, then sued the London bank, when it had been endorsed, for conversion. However, Austrian law applied to the negotiation and, despite the forgery, a bona fide holder for value obtained a good title. Austrian law was applied and Embiricos succeeded.

Characterisation

Characterisation is the least well-known factor but it cannot be ignored. This is where the laws of one country regard a transaction as being of a different legal character from what it is considered to be by the law of another country. For example, "prescription," the loss of right as a result of the elapse of time, is regarded by German law as a matter of property and thus governed by the law of its situs (*i.e.* Germany) but by English law it is regarded as a matter of procedure, being concerned as to the limitation of a right of action and determined by the rules of the country where the action is brought. Again an exchange control regulation may be regarded as an expropriation or as a revenue law or even as a law flowing from a treaty. Thus whether it is governed by the law of a particular country may depend on the type of act that the courts concerned consider it to be. According to the way in which it has been classified or characterised those courts decide whether—according to their rules of conflict of laws—to apply the law of their own or of another country.

II

The Primary Banking Functions

It has already been suggested that jurisdiction in its two aspects of where an action is going to be brought and of where a judgment, if obtained, can be enforced, is a dominant factor. At the same time it is acknowledged that the law that the particular court is likely to apply will be selected on principles that themselves have a consistent basis. The courts of each country may have different rules of conflict of laws but there are certain common features, some born of practical necessity, such as the application of the law of the country concerned where title to land is in dispute. A reference was also made to "characterisation," that is as to the basis upon which courts of one country classify acts as being concerned with a particular matter. For example, the courts of one country may regard a matter concerning a mortgage secured on land as coming within the classification of an immoveable and thus governed by the law of the country where the land is situated whereas the courts of another country may classify such a mortgage as being "a debt" and therefore subject to the law of the country in which the debtor resided. Similarly, the loss of a right of action by lapse of time may be regarded as a substantive matter involving the law of the country to which the right related whereas in another country, such incidentally as England, it would be regarded as a matter of procedure and governed by the law of the country where the action is being heard—in the case of England, by the Limitation Acts.

THE PRACTICAL PROBLEMS

Inevitably where—as in this case—the object of a book, is essentially to be of practical help the balance of any presentation suffers. To deal with a subject on a symmetrical basis means inevitably covering instances that not only have not happened but which are unlikely to happen. For this reason the topics that I propose to consider may be in the nature of a miscellany. They have the virtue nevertheless of having occurred (or threatened to occur) in the practice of foreign banking. This facet does not however preclude grouping of problems that will be associated with the familiar functions of banking. The major problems are: the primary banking functions; the secondary banking functions; and Government intervention. Within the first category it is proposed to consider the paying banker; the collecting banker; the type of customer; the lending banker; and security. In each case, of course, the subjects will be examined from the standpoint of a banker in the United Kingdom who does mainly foreign business.

The paying banker

Here, perhaps in contradistinction to many other facets, is an activity, which is simple and in which the position of the banker engaged in foreign business is reasonably certain. It is pertinent, although no doubt unnecessary, to state that a cheque has two qualities that spring from different sources: it is a bill of exchange and has all the qualities of that document unless they are deliberately eliminated by one of the parties; also, it is the document that causes the banker-customer contract to come into operation. Just as a drawee may be under no obligation to accept or pay a bill drawn upon him, the banker is often not under any obligation to pay a cheque. I am, however, able to confirm that very little, if any, of the rules contained in the Bills of Exchange Act 1882 regarding the conflict of laws[1] will concern you in relation to the payment of cheques. The reason for this relative simplicity is because the contract between the banker and customer, where the banker is in this country, is governed by English law.[2] In the last chapter when we alluded in general terms to the question of what law governed a particular transaction reference was made to the intentions of the parties. If these are not specific the courts will either ascertain from the surrounding circumstances what the parties were presumed to intend or will apply the law of the country with which the transaction is most closely associated. On any basis it is English law where the account is with a branch of a bank, in England, whether incorporated here or not. This means that the obligation as to the payment of cheques will be construed in accordance with English law. The protection given by the Bills of Exchange Act (section 60 and section 80) will apply as also will the relief contained in section I of the Cheques Act 1957, notwithstanding that the payee is abroad or the presenting banker is a bank established abroad. It will be seen that the Committee of London Clearing Bankers did not differentiate in their Circular as to the duty of paying bankers regarding cheques payable to persons abroad. In the case of *Embiricos* v. *Anglo-Austrian Bank*, noted in the last chapter, it was the presenting banker, to whom the cheque had been indorsed after being cashed in Austria, who was sued. It was recognised that the paying banker was protected despite the forged indorsement. For the most part the paying banker will be in no different position, apart form Exchange Control

---

[1] Section 72.
[2] This is beyond doubt and is confirmed and illustrated by cases in Dicey, Conflict of Laws (10th ed.) p. 536.

requirements, when paying a cheque drawn by a customer resident abroad, from that in which he would be if the cheque had been drawn by a customer resident in the United Kingdom. Of course, if there had been a special arrangement between the customer and the paying banker such special circumstances could affect the result. For example, London bankers may often pay drafts drawn upon them by a banker abroad under advice; that is to say the agreement or course of business between the two bankers as to whether the receipt of the advice is a pre-condition of payment will be the determining factor. Customers often approach bankers to seek special arrangements regarding the operation of a banking account. Whether these are acceptable to a banker depend very much upon the measure of administrative inconvenience likely to be caused. At one time residents in certain countries occasionally approached bankers wishing cheques to be paid only if signed in a certain way, perhaps with full names instead of initials, so that if cheques were issued under duress and signed they would not be paid despite the genuine signature. This was fraught with possible difficulty and, generally speaking, not acceptable. It may be apt to mention that the whole question of a signature of a cheque under duress does not appear to have been clarified at English law, namely, whether, the genuine signature was the mandate and binding on the customer or whether he could seek relief. In another instance, where a forged cheque drawn on an English banker is paid abroad by a paying agent the question arises of whether the customer's negligence, if a good defence for a paying banker in the country of payment, will enable the English banker to refuse reimbursement; in this instance there is again the impact of special circumstances.

The completion of payment has been considered by the courts in a number of cases in recent years. At one time its achievement depended on communication to the recipient[3]; now it appears to be dependent upon the time that bankers debit one account and credit another as in the case of *The Brimnes*.[4] The case of *Momm* v. *Barclays Bank International* [1977] Q.B. 790 is illuminating in that the decision depended on the agreement between the parties attributing the value date "26 June 1974" which was the day on which the insolvency of Herstatt became known internationally. A quirk was evidenced in the case of *The Chikuma* [1981] 1 W.L.R. 314 where money was regarded as not having been paid on time because the account holder in Italy, the recipient, could not claim interest until the amount had been held for two days. In *The Laconia* [1977] A.C. 850 it was held that a recipient banker although receiving money as an agent had no authority to bind his principal (that is his customer) to accept early receipt.

---

[3] *Rekstin* v. *Severo* [1933] 1 K.B. 47.
[4] [1975] Q.B. 929.

Sometimes the simple position flowing from the application of English law can be slightly bedevilled by the more difficult problem of jurisdiction. The courts of some countries, *e.g.* France, were willing to assume jurisdiction in respect of any claim of a French national even although the defendant was outside France and the subject matter of the litigation unconnected with France.[5] Thus a French national resident in France could in theory bring an action in France against an English banker regarding the payment of cheques. However, there are a number of reasons why this would have no attraction. In the first place it is likely that the French court would apply English law; secondly, enforcement here may well be resisted successfully. Above all the whole basis of enforcement is reciprocity and comity, which would cause the courts in France to discourage such proceedings. In a less remote way the English paying banker may appear to be concerned as to the operation of garnishee orders resultant upon foreign judgments because they may be enforceable here. This however is not very likely. In *Martin* v. *Nadel* [1906] 2 K.B. 26 the courts refused to enforce against a London branch by garnishee order a judgment obtained against its Head Office in Berlin. Similarly in *Richardson* v. *Richardson* [1927] P. 228 a judgment creditor was unsuccessful in attempting to get an English judgment extended to attach balances of the judgment debtor at branches of the bank abroad. Where, however, on an *English* judgment, after the defendant had submitted to a hearing in the English courts, a Czechoslovakian bank obtained a garnishee order in respect of an obligation that had arisen abroad, it was enforced because the view was taken that there was no danger of the debtor having to pay twice, that is in Prague as well as in London.[6] In *Choice Investments Ltd.* v. *Jeromnimon* [1981] 1 Q.B. 225 a garnishment of currency was upheld.

Nevertheless, these contingencies are remote. To summarise, where no special arrangements have been made the paying banker can pay cheques of a foreign national or resident on the same basis as those of an English customer so long as he observes any exchange control restrictions. (The latter subject is considered in the last chapter.)

We are reminded of the international aspect by the case of *R.* v. *Lovitt* [1912] A.C. 213 where, because a deceased customer had his banking account at a branch, for the purpose of succession duty it was regarded as situated there, despite the customer having died in Nova Scotia. Again the Arab-Israeli War gave rise to the case of *Arab Bank Ltd.* v. *Barclays (D.C.O.)* [1954] A.C. 495 when the credit balance at Barclays Jerusalem although surviving, was held not

---

[5] This is now affected by the Brussels Treaty incorporated in the Civil Jurisdictions and Judgments Act 1982 for which see Appendix A.
[6] *Swiss Bank Corporation* v. *Bohemische Bank* [1923] 1 K.B. 673.

recoverable because it was payable to the custodian by the local law. In *Rossano* v. *Manufacturers Life Insurance Co.* [1963] 2 Q.B. 352 three endowment life policies had been established in Ontario in 1940 by an Egyptian, the premiums being paid in Cairo; the policies matured in March 1960 and two were to be payable in London by demand drafts and the other in New York. Egyptian tax authorities attempted to attach the balance of monies held to meet the policies because there was an option under the policy for payment to have been in Egypt. English courts declined to assist in the collection of a foreign tax claim and by Egyptian law the proper law of the contract was disregarded. Also relevant is the case of *Power Curber* v. *National Bank of Kuwait SAK* [1981] 1 W.L.R. 1233 where a documentary credit payable in North Carolina was held to be governed by the law of that territory because it was with that territory that it had its closest connection; this was despite a decision in Kuwait staying payment. Payment by a bank is also concerned with the case of *Banque des Marchands de Moscou (Koupetschesky), Re Royal Exchange Assurance* v. *Liquidator* [1952] 1 All E.R. 1269, where the balance claimed was held to have been extinguished by the Russian legislation of 1917.

The collecting banker

Traditionally the collecting banker has been regarded as being *either* an agent for collection *or* a holder in his own right, often a holder in due course. Now it appears that whenever there is a debit balance this itself is sufficient value for a banker to become a holder in due course of a cheque paid in[7] irrespective of whether he has given value by paying against uncleared effects, exchanging the cheque for cash or receiving it in specific reduction of a loan or overdraft. However, for there to be a "holder in due course" the cheque will have had to be negotiated in accordance with the law of the place where the negotiation took place. To claim as a holder the banker will be dependent upon the negotiability of the cheque and upon its valid negotiation. He is concerned with it as a bill of exchange. The liability of the drawer is ascertained by the law of the place where it is drawn. Yet generally where a cheque has come from abroad the banker will be collecting for a foreign bank. He will be the agent of the foreign banker and will hardly ever be concerned with his rights against prior parties. He will almost invariably be able to resort to his banking correspondent as his principal for whom he is collecting (or perhaps as a transferor by delivery if the cheque is payable to bearer) as well as to the preceding holder. In practice this situation has been so untroubled that little contention and almost no litigation has emerged since the case of *Importers Company*

---

[7] *Keever* v. *Midland Bank Ltd.* [1967] Ch. 182; *Barclays Bank Ltd.* v. *Astley Industrial Trust* [1970] 2 Q.B. 527.

Ltd. v. *Westminster Bank Ltd.* [1927] 2 K.B. 297. In that case the Westminster Bank collected a cheque crossed "Account Payee" for a German bank; the cheque had been stolen and the endorsement forged, so that the customer of the German bank, although innocent had no title to the cheque. The drawers sued the Westminster Bank but they were unsuccessful because the court held that the German bank were customers of the Westminster Bank and that they were entitled to the statutory protection (at that time section 82 of the Bills of Exchange Act). Further, it was held that the Westminster Bank had discharged its duty of care by paying over the proceeds to the banker by whom the cheque had been crossed to the Westminster Bank as agent for collection, despite the crossing "Account Payee" which in domestic banking usually necessitates the crediting of the payee's account.

Where, however, instead of collecting a cheque, payable here, on behalf of a foreign banker the English banker is collecting a cheque payable abroad, normally drawn in foreign currency, for the credit of a domestic customer the position is different. The English banker is then the principal of the foreign banker through whom he effects the collection. Generally in relation to all matters carried out through an agent, the bank is responsible for the default of his agent.[8] This is upon the principle that the banker like any other agent is responsible for the default of his sub-agent. This may not be so where the principal specifically directs the agent to use a particular sub-agent.[9] Yet it is wise, however, for a collecting banker to provide by arrangement with his customer that he will not be responsible for the defects of the agent banker nominated by the customer. In order not to create offence it is desirable for these stipulations to be general regarding all agents used—or at least regarding all agents nominated by the customers. In the case of *Calico Printers Association* v. *Barclays Bank Ltd.*[10] the disavowal was contained in the form giving the instructions.[11]

There is a more embarrassing responsibility that might arise out of collecting a cheque for a customer who has no title. This may have been done within the requirements of section 4 of the Cheques Act but the collecting banker may be sued in the courts of the country where payment was effected. Strictly one would expect the foreign court to apply English law to the collection, since the transaction fundamentally giving rise to an action such as conversion was sub-

---

[8] *MacKersy* v. *Ramsays, Bonars & Co.* (1843) 8 E.R. 628.
[9] Compare an Australian case *S. A. Joseph & Richard Ltd.* v. *Lindley* (1905) 3 C.L.R. 28, where the principal specifically agreed the delegation by the agent.
[10] (1931) 145 L.T. 51. The validity of such a provision may now be adversely affected by the Unfair Contract Terms Act 1977.
[11] It has to be borne in mind that a proviso eliminating the bankers responsibility may be subjected to the requirement of reasonableness by the Unfair Contract Terms Act 1977.

ject to English law, *i.e.* the relationship between the customer and his English banker was an English contract. It is just possible, although unlikely, that a different view would be taken by the foreign court. In addition the enforcement of such a judgment here might be opposed if there had been false evidence of English law before the foreign court, although its enforcement against the assets of the English collecting banker in the foreign jurisdiction could not be thwarted. Of more concern is the responsibility that the English collecting banker may have to his foreign banking correspondent through whom he collects. Rather than indulge in litigation the foreign party who has been deprived may seek recovery through pressing his bankers to redebit the English banker for whose customer the cheque was collected. For example in the United States by the Uniform Commercial Code,[12] the collecting banker warrants to the paying banker that he has a good title to the item, that he has no knowledge that drawer's signature is unauthorised, and that the cheque has not been materially altered. This can mean that, if the English banker's customer's title is bad, or any of the other circumstances mentioned obtain, the English banker can be re-debited. The United Kingdom banker is of course responsible for the validity of endorsements. There are a number of exceptions to the provisions permitting a reclaiming, including the safe-guarding of the position of a holder in due course. Nevertheless the possible risk has been indicated, to collect a cheque for $50,000 for a man worth £500.

It is a fair conclusion that the collecting banker is seldom likely to be embarrassed except that he should regard the risks involved in collecting a large foreign currency draft or cheque for a man of straw as being similar to those involved in the negotiation of the same cheque. If it were desired to eliminate the other remote risk with a large third party cheque (of the liability for conversion or on some similar ground under foreign law) the authority of the payee would of course suffice.

The type of customer

This subject is obviously very wide and comments within this volume cannot be comprehensive. The immediate aspect arising is the extent to which a particular type of customer coming from abroad or having associations with a foreign country may be unable to deal with an English bank in the same way as could an English customer. Closely associated with this question is whether the difference in capacity is likely to be material in banking. For a large part fortunately this is not the case. Nevertheless there are instances to which attention should be drawn.

Whilst English rules as to conflict of laws are not beyond contro-

---

[12] Section 4–207.

versy on the subject, the better view is certainly that the capacity of a customer must conform to the requirements of English law, although he is unlikely to have any greater capacity because he is in this country than he would have had elsewhere. There is one old case, *Male* v. *Roberts* (1800) 3 Esp. 163, by which it was suggested that the contractual capacity was governed solely by the laws of the country where the contract arose. The better view is now, however, that a party's capacity to contract is governed by the law governing the contract generally, that is to say the law of the country with which the contract is most substantially connected.[13] Obviously for all practical reasons this will be England and, therefore, there is much to be said for the argument that English law will govern the capacity of a customer to open a banking account here. The sort of problem one encounters is whether the Corporation established abroad is restricted by its own constitution and the laws of the country where it is established. Of lesser significance are the problems arising from someone being under age by the laws of his own country or being regarded by those laws as subject to control. This would arise in the event of someone being *non compos mentis*. In some places also, *e.g.* in France, there are special forms of incapacity quite unassociated with insanity. There is the category of the "prodigal" where someone is irresponsible or perhaps profligate and his affairs are, therefore, put under the control of a curator. On occasions that person wishes to open a banking account in England and his ability so to do appears to be unimpaired because his curator is not recognised here.[14] It is proposed to deal with this problem of capacity in three groups, the first of which is the most important: corporations, infants, other persons of limited capacity.

Corporations

As indicated already, the capacity of a limited company to contract may be restricted by both the law of the place where the company is established and the law of the country where the transaction takes place. That is to say, a foreign company opening an English banking account must certainly conform with the requirements of its own constitution and, it is generally thought, with the law of England. Before, however, examining this aspect further there is an earlier point to be borne in mind. That is that the very existence of a foreign Corporation is determined by the law of the country where it is established. Relevantly, in the case of the *National Bank of Greece and Athens* v. *Metliss* [1958] A.C. 509, it was held that whether a company had been effectively amalgamated with another company had

---

[13] *Charron* v. *Montreal Trust Co.* (1959) 15 D.L.R. 240; approved in Dicey, Conflict of Laws (10th ed.), p. 783.
[14] *Re Selot's Trusts* [1902] 1 Ch. 488.

to be determined by the law of Greece where both companies were established. Similarly, if a foreign company has a branch in England, the branch cannot initiate legal proceedings here after the company has been dissolved in the country where its Head Office is established.

Once having decided that the company exists, it is necessary to distinguish between the power of the company and the authority of those signing on behalf of the company. The rights of shareholders among themselves and the authority of directors and other officials of a foreign company are ascertained by the constitution of the foreign company as interpreted by the laws of the country of its incorporation. For example, in the case of *Banco de Bilbao* v. *Sancha* [1938] 2 K.B. 176, a decree of the Spanish Government appointed two new directors. The two new directors were held to be entitled to control all the operations of the London branch, just as much as they were able to deal with the assets in Spain. With a credit account there is unlikely to be any difficulty for an English banker. He will see the company's constitution. In practice, he is likely to have verification from the company's foreign bankers as to the genuineness of the signatures upon which he is to act. It is little more to ask the foreign banking correspondents to confirm that the persons concerned are authorised to act on behalf of the company. If, however, the powers of the company, or for that matter any other form of foreign corporation, are restricted, then it is wise and probably necessary, for there to be confirmation obtained that the company has, for example, power to carry on business outside its own territory. In virtually all cases this is likely to be so.

There are instances where a foreign company is less inhibited than an English company. To take an example from the Australian Companies Act 1961, by which Austrialian companies are forbidden to act beyond their powers. However, unlike the effect of similar *ultra vires* activity of an English company, the Australian company is bound notwithstanding.[15] The main effect in Australia of a company acting *ultra vires* is that a member of the company or perhaps another interested party is able to obtain an injunction to prevent a continuance of such activity. What then, it may be asked, is the position of an English banker who is concerned with an Australian company? Can he ignore the *ultra vires* implications because by Australian law the company is liable? The better view is that the Australian company could not be sued here; because advantage could be taken of the rules of English law in respect of the *"ultra vires"* activity.

At this stage it is also appropriate to remind bankers that if a foreign company has an office here then it has to effect registration

---

[15] Australian Companies Act 1961, s.20. In England the position as to *ultra vires* Acts of a company are subject to the validating provisions of the European Communities Act 1972, s.1.

as an "Oversea Company."[16] As part of this registration it is necessary to deliver to the Registrar of Joint Stock Companies a copy of the constitution and other appropriate information regarding the officers of the company. In addition an address has to be given where the company can be served in the event of litigation. There are a number of other provisions in Part XXIII of the Companies Act relating to an oversea companies, perhaps the most important of which is the need to register mortgages and charges that would be registerable if the company itself were an English company.[17]

The infant customer

The term "infant" is used in its widest sense as including anyone who has not full contractual capacity because he has not reached a particular age. This includes *e.g.* both categories recognised by Scots law, pupils under the age of 14 in the case of boys and under the age of 12 in the case of girls, as well as minors between those ages and 21. The ages of majority vary from time to time and place to place. Recently we in England, have reduced that age from 21 to 18; in Turkey it is the same, except that a boy marrying at 17 or a girl marrying at 15 is regarded as attaining majority and that *anyone* may be so classified at 15 upon application to the court and consent of his parents. Before considering the implications of foreign law it is well to note the principle relating to *credit* accounts obtaining in England. The recognised view is that an infant may open a banking account and, by receipt of the balance or the drawing of cheques that are paid, estops himself from claiming the monies that were held on his behalf by the banker.[18] Concurrently, there is the basic principle that the infant must be able to understand the nature of the transaction; this is in each instance a question of fact as to which a banker probably depends on the extent of contrary notice.

It is reasonable to regard the same position as applicable to English credit banking accounts of infants who are either resident abroad or who are foreign nationals. That is to say that, because the normal intention of both banker and customer is that English law shall apply and because an English court, at all events, will accept as applicable the law of the country with which the contract has the closest connection. Thus English law will obtain. Because of the position obtaining here relating to the conduct of credit accounts by infants the contractual position may not be vital; it will however

---

[16] Companies Act 1985, s.409 *et. seq.*
[17] In *South India Shipping Corp.* v. *Export-Import Bank of Korea* [1985] 1 W.L.R. 585, the defendant bank had its main business in Korea but was held to have a place of business in London where the service was made and was held to be good although the London address was not registered.
[18] *Cf.* Paget, *Law of Banking* (10th ed.), p. 30.

affect the burden of proof as to whether the nature of the transaction is understood; that is to say, if the foreign age of majority is held not to be applicable, the banker has to prove understanding which burden he would escape if the child was deemed to be of age. With borrowing accounts, to which special reference will be made shortly, the capacity to contract may be more material. For example, is someone, by whose national law he does not attain contractual capacity until 25, able to contract in this country when he is 18? Or, is someone (a young married Turk perhaps) whose national law gives him majority at 17 able to bind himself at 17 here? And, again, is the position the same if the customer never sets foot in England but makes all the arrangements by telephone or by post and invariably draws his cheques from abroad? These questions are however hardly material in relation to a credit account in that a banker merely has to establish that he has paid money away at the behest of the infant and not to establish the benefit that the infant has received (unless the principles of the *Selangor* case[19] are going to be applied or extended against banks to an inordinate degree). The problems will be specially relevant in relation to the rights of the lending banker.

Mental incapacity

It is inconceivable that the rights, *vis-à-vis* his banker, of a customer who is mentally incapacitated will be any different because he is a national of a foreign country or has his permanent home there. The nature of the contract is that the customer is bound if the banker has no notice of the mental incapacity.[20] This, admittedly difficult to establish (although also sometimes to refute!) does not vary, like the age of majority from country to country. It is a medical fact and, presumably, determined on common ground. It is hard to visualise someone being regarded as "sane" by the "law" of France and "insane" by the "law" of England. The legal consequences may vary. Here again, however, to deal with someone knowing his incapacity is attempting to benefit from principles that one cannot imagine a civilised court enforcing beyond the extent to which the incapacitated person has benefitted. Yet to suffer by reason of such insanity without having notice is also equally difficult to envisage. What may legally be notice or benefit may vary according to the place where the contract comes into force but, neither in banking, nor in other mercantile contracts, is there anything on record to suggest that *other* than English law would decide the rights of an English banker against his *non compos mentis* customer.

The question of obtaining a quittance or discharge for a credit balance may be a different matter. Where a receiver is appointed in

---

[19] *Selangor United Rubber Estates* v. *Cradock* [1968] 1 W.L.R. 1555.
[20] *Imperial Loan Co.* v. *Stone* [1892] 1 Q.B. 599.

the United Kingdom he can give a valid receipt. In turn he has certain duties to pay over monies to a foreign curator, but this is a subject for his discretion or more probably for the discretion of the Court of Protection. If there is no receiver appointed in the United Kingdom, there is no doubt that the curator appointed in the country of the customer's domicile can give a good discharge.[21] Whether this can be obtained from a similar official appointed in the place where the customer has only a residence as distinct from a domicile (technically a permanent home which he evinced no intention, before becoming *non compos mentis*, of leaving permanently) the position is not free from doubt. The solution is to pay over only at the direction of an English court, although this may entail paying costs[22] of the application.

Married women

The accounts of married women are today, of course, by English law treated exactly in the same way as those of any other adult person and, but for one aspect, would not have merited separate comment. This is the possibility that a married woman may come from a country where the principle of *communio bonorum* obtains. This may mean that either by reason of election, or of failing to elect otherwise, at the time of her marriage her property becomes that also of her husband. If the matrimonial home is still in that country, then monies received for her account may be part of the "joint" assets. Even if she is living here indefinitely money received from abroad could be part of those assets. Now the contract of banker and customer is admittedly governed by English law as is the capacity of an account holder. For this reason the banker need not be concerned merely because of this possibility of "joint" property, which the English courts regard as the property of a trust.[23] However, if an English banker receives specific notice, which occasionally may happen, he has to regard it as notice that the property is trust property, for which, after such notice, it is doubtful whether his customer alone can give him a good discharge. The occasions are rare and becoming more so because of the lesser frequency with which foreign brides are willing to agree to such a system, if they have an opportunity to declare otherwise.

The lending banker

So far we have made little reference to the facet of our subject that we indicated was, from the legal standpoint, the most important:

---

[21] *Didisheim* v. *London Westminster Bank* [1900] 2 Ch. 15.
[22] *Pelegrin* v. *Coutts & Co.* [1915] 1 Ch. 696.
[23] *De Nicols* v. *Curlier* [1900] A.C. 21.

"jurisdiction."[24] With a credit account the likelihood anticipated in the main was of being sued here although reference was made to the collecting of a draft and the possibility of an action being brought in a foreign country against an English banker. The lending banker is concerned with the thought that if his customer is not carrying on business here an action would probably have to be commenced abroad, and that in any event the need to satisfy a judgment obtained may mean that an action has to be brought outside this country. For these reasons the banker in the United Kingdom will frequently seek some cover. This may take the form of tangible security or it may be a guarantee from a banker abroad, whose financial standing is beyond cavil. What is more, the prospect of a settlement of any dispute will also be much better if there is the intermediate factor of the local banker. Yet again the close acquaintance with the customer's current position is likely to be facilitated where watch is being kept by the banker in the country where the principal (or parent) activity is being pursued. Sometimes this guarantee is offered by the parent company of a corporate borrower whose financial standing is so strong that it will be acceptable to a banker in the United Kingdom. Such circumstances occur more usually where the subsidiary or associate company is incorporated as an English company. Where there is a foreign borrower, one general principle, stemming from English law, is that it is safer to take an indemnity rather than a guarantee, because of the possible effect of incapacity of the principal borrower. In addition an indemnity may even be drawn to cover the contingency of supervening illegality. If *e.g.* the repayment of an English banker is made illegal by a moratorium, repayment could be obtained from the English assets of the indemnifier because the banker-customer contract is governed by English law. It is true that the English courts are hesitant to enforce a contract which it is illegal for one party to perform but it is suggested that this would not extend to an indemnity given specifically against the contingency.

In discussing lending it is proposed to confine the examination to what, some years ago, one could have described as true "deposit banking." That is to say the indebtedness is repayable on demand. Banks, of course, provide longer term finance in many ways. Export credit finance, documentary credit facilities, investment participation are but a few examples, the second of which will be touched upon later. Traditional bank lending to a foreign borrower is, generally speaking, likely to be for an enterprise operating here; otherwise the point immediately arises as to why finance cannot be obtained in the foreign country concerned. It may be that the proposition relates to a specific purpose for which finance abroad is not available. However, if there is an associate English company, involved in some way

---

[24] See Chap. 1, p. 3.

in the contract, it will be likely to be interested in finance being provided. Such company may be willing to arrange, by way of security, to pay proceeds of sale or instalments due on a contract to the English lending banker.

When examining the limited capacity of the foreign body reference was made to its importance to the lending banker. Where an English banker is looking to reimbursement from a foreign source then this aspect is vital, whether he expects to recover direct from a foreign borrower or from a guarantor. For example, guarantees by United States corporations for subsidiaries are normally within a corporation's capacity; but it is necessary to seek formal confirmation from an American lawyer practising in the state of incorporation if a guarantee is being taken for the liabilities of a borrower who has no such filial connection. Most people here will be familiar with the habit of United States banks overcoming the problem by establishing a clean letter of credit.

It is, of course, very unlikely that an English banker will become involved in claims against private individuals who are foreign nationals or domiciled abroad. He will normally merely wish to ensure that he obtains a good discharge for a credit balance and, if he has doubts time will usually be available for those doubts to be set at rest. Even if he is faced with a cheque presented for payment if there are doubts as to the capacity of the drawer he can refuse payment, pending confirmation, without there being any real risk of damages. Where the borrowing customer is a corporation or a limited partnership of which there are a number of varieties established abroad, the lending banker will be advised either to seek cover from a foreign banker or confirmation from the banker as to the capacity to enter into engagements, whether it be by way of guarantee or as a borrower direct.

Securities

For facilities provided to home customers, and occasionally to foreign residents, a variety of securities associated with foreign countries are sometimes offered to English bankers. Naturally, such type of security is normally taken as a last resort. It may be that a debt has become doubtful and that, for what worth, any kind of security is better than none; or it may be that the banker particularly wishes to assist and requires additional security or would be inclined to help without any security but accepts a foreign security without being much concerned as to its validity.

For example, foreign land can normally be mortgaged only in accordance with the formalities of the country where it is situated. Nevertheless if an informal charge is given here an English court will force the mortgagor to do all that is necessary to enable the English mortgagee to realise his security, so long as that course is not illegal by the law of the country where the land is situated. Floating charges are now valid to a limited effect in Scotland (where incidentally a more modern enactment exists covering[25] many of the points that have caused controversy here for years) but a recent case illustrates the difficulty of the problem.[26] A Scottish company with a place of business in England also granted a banker a floating charge over its freehold property in England and its heritable property in Scotland. Particulars of the first were registered in England and of the second in Scotland pursuant to the Companies Acts 1948–1961. It was held that particulars of the charge on the English property should have been registered in Scotland also (for which purpose an extension of time was granted). However, in relation to the proceeds of the land in the hands of an English liquidator or receiver an English court would have held the charge to be valid. There would thus have been a conflict of jurisdiction. A similar difficulty may make it unwise to take undated unstamped transfers together with the deposit of the share certificate and an equitable form of charge where the company, whose shares are mortgaged has a Scottish registration. If the mortgagor dies appointing a Scottish executor and there is an insolvency, it is difficult to see how the registrar of the Scottish company can refuse to accept the executor's claim to the shares. Similarly, it seems, a trustee in bankruptcy cannot be refused. The place where shares are physically may also effect the validity of security. In India, *e.g.* it is illegal to sell shares, the subject of a pledge, without giving at least 21 days' notice. An English form of bank charge, which provides for sale on demand, or even sometimes for sale without notice, is probably effective, subject to the variation. This is normally an aspect on which enquiry should be made but if the securities are in India, deposited by an English bank, it may be that the point will not be raised by either banker if the charge is taken in London. Bearer shares are subject to the law of the place where they are physically,[27] as it appears also are shares transferable by endorsement of a certificate.[28] These points of law have arisen principally in relation to the problem of whether estate duty is payable. Yet the efficacy of an attempt to obtain a charge by a banker will be dependent on satisfying the court where any action has to be brought. Usually such court will apply the relative law on the above principles, *but* the contrary contingency is always a risk unless control of the security in deliverable form is available to the mortgagee banker or to his agent. For this reason where shares registerable abroad are taken as security it is advisable to complete the

---

[25] Companies (Floating Charges and Receivers) Scotland Act 1972. Re-enacted in the Companies Act 1985, ss.462 *et. seq.*
[26] *Re Amalgamated Securities Ltd.* [1967] S.C. 54.
[27] *Winans* v. *Attorney General* [1910] A.C. 27.
[28] *Stern* v. *R.* [1896] 1 Q.B. 211.

registration in the name of mortgagee banker's nominees at the time of the mortgage.

A *life policy* is subject to the law of the place of its head office, although usually this will have little unexpected effect. Companies whose head office is in Edinburgh usually, *e.g.*, issue English policies specifically subject to English law from London. The law controlling the policy can sometimes have an adverse effect on a mortgagee. For example,[29] even although the husband and wife jointly agree to charge a Scottish policy issued under the Married Women's (Scotland) Property Act, the charge, unlike a similar charge on an English policy, will be invalid. To illustrate the position further, in the case of *Pender* v. *Commercial Bank of Scotland*[30] a policy was issued in Edinburgh under the English statute, the Married Women's Property Act of 1882, being issued by an English insurance company. It was charged in Scotland by both the husband and wife to a Scottish bank, the assignment being in Scottish form. The court decided the issue on the question of whether the parties intended the policy to be assignable. Here there seems to be the possibility of different decisions being given by an English, as distinct from a Scottish court.

Conclusion

In this chapter we have concluded:

(1) the paying banker need not concern himself with foreign aspects;
(2) the collecting banker must bear in mind one important risk, that of negotiating sizeable foreign drafts, *e.g.* payable in U.S.A., for men of straw because of the possibility of recourse through an agent banker;
(3) limitations of customers powers will rarely concern a banker when an account is in credit although the delegation, say, by a company to its officials will have to accord with the constitution of a foreign corporation;
(4) the lending banker is concerned with capacity. His practical solution is often a foreign bank indemnity;
(5) securities taken abroad or which may be regarded as situated abroad should be transferred as far as possible to the lending banker or his agent.

---

[29] *Scottish Life Assurance Co.* v. *John Donald* [1901] S.L.T. 200.
[30] [1940] S.L.T. 306.

III

Insolvency and The Secondary Functions

In the first chapter considerable emphasis was placed upon the importance in practice of jurisdiction: where an action could be brought and where judgment, if obtained, could be enforced. It may well be claimed that when looking at the legal implications from the standpoint of the British banker doing foreign business involving the primary banking functions, there was comparatively little allusion to jurisdiction. More in fact was said as to the law that would apply to particular aspects of the banker–customer relationship. This was because for the most part the law relating to the banker–customer contract is so overwhelmingly accepted as being that of the country where the account is kept.[1] The same principle would be applied by most courts. For reasons of convenience, if for none other, the courts of most civilised countries would apply English law to an argument about an English banking account. It is true that there may be a temptation to sue where there are assets, yet there is no likelihood of any different ultimate decision being obtained from that which would be given by an English court. In fact, even in countries with whom there is *no* arrangement for the reciprocal enforcement of judgments, it is often easier to start with an English judgment and seek its enforcement following examination by the court. However, insolvency, the next subject that we propose considering gives full play to the significance of jurisdiction.[2]

INSOLVENCY

The international problems of insolvency affect bankers in several ways: the attempt to bankrupt an individual who has left the country; the attempt to collect foreign assets of an English bankrupt; the question of whether a good discharge can be obtained by paying a credit balance to a foreign trustee; the priorities of competing bankruptcies in different countries. Whilst "bankruptcy" relates by English law to the individual only, the term is also applied in some countries, *e.g.* the United States, to insolvent companies. At all events many of the legal problems arising internationally relating to

---

[1] *R.* v. *Lovitt* [1912] A.C. 212.
[2] For the past 10 years there have been proposals for British participation in a bankruptcy convention which is still under discussion.

the bankruptcy of an individual also exist, with some variations, in relation to the insolvent liquidations of corporations, especially in respect of proofs of debt.

The insolvent who goes abroad and leaves assets here is perhaps the least difficult to deal with from a *legal* aspect, although, practically speaking, because he is in business here, the amounts of claims with which bankers are concerned may be larger and arise more frequently than where facilities are sought by a foreign resident. Residence abroad of a customer other than another banker, is still basically a deterrent to the lending banker. English law gives plenty of opportunity for recovery to the banker who has lent money and then found that his customer has left the country, unless the assets have also been removed abroad: even then, so long as those assets are traceable, and not in the form of a numbered account in Switzerland, it is often possible to recover them. There are several bases upon which the debtor may be made bankrupt here despite his having left the country. To begin with, any of the first three acts of bankruptcy on which a petition may be founded: assignment for the benefit of creditors, fraudulent conveyance and fraudulent preferences are all statutorily valid if committed "in England or elsewhere."[3] Again, of its nature, "departing out of England to defeat or to delay creditors,"[4] although requiring the establishment of a presumption of intention relates to foreign residence. What is more, substituted service will be allowed by the court although the debtor is out of the country.[5] It is true that, normally for bankruptcy proceedings to be started the debtor must have carried on business or have been ordinarily resident here within the previous 12 months. This is, of course, the basis that we are considering. When it gets too oppressive here the debtor goes abroad. Some of his assets do not go with him and are traced. These he is likely to have to disgorge. In fact, if a man had been trading here and left the country without having paid his debts he was deemed to have committed an act of bankruptcy.[6] In the case of *Theophile* v. *The Solicitor General*,[7] the debtor, a foreign national domiciled abroad had carried on business in England for some years. He then sold up and went to Eire leaving a tax obligation. It was held that he was "out of England" and

---

[3] The Bankruptcy Act 1914, s. (1) (*a*), (*b*) and (*c*). This section was repealed by the Insolvency Act 1985, Sched. 10, Pt. III.
[4] *Ibid*, s.(1)(*d*).
[5] *Re Urquhart* (1890) 24 Q.B.D. 723.
[6] *Ex p. Goater* (1874) 30 L.T. 620. The necessary institution is not difficult to set up. At this stage it is appropriate to refer to the new insolvency law equating the proximity of insolvency of individuals to that of companies and removing the eight acts of bankruptcy which is not expected to be effective until after the middle of December 1986 at the earliest. The application of the new law is conjectural and in relation to decisions based on the repealed legislation the position is dependant upon the new proposed Bankruptcy Convention still under E.E.C. discussion.
[7] [1950] A.C. 186.

"remained out of England" and, that within the terms of section (1) (i) (d) of the Bankruptcy Act, this was an act of bankruptcy. The necessity is to be aware of assets of any kind that are likely to afford a realisable source of repayment.

Insolvent companies

Where, as may perhaps more frequently be the case, the debtor is a corporation the position is also simple. If the debtor is an English limited company no comment is necessary. If the company is incorporated abroad the first question is whether the company is an "oversea company."[8] If a company registered here is controlled by persons resident abroad or who are foreign nationals it may nevertheless be wound up here in the same way as any other English company: by its members if it is solvent or by its creditors, with or without an order of the court, if it is insolvent. This is despite the fact that by reason of its control from abroad it is regarded for tax purposes as resident abroad.[9] Moreover by reason of such foreign residence or control an English registered company may be subjected by the courts within the foreign country to a distribution of the assets according to local rules. It may also be that, as would happen here, authority would be given to the liquidator to collect assets that are outside the national boundaries. It seems further, that such foreign administration of the assets of an English company would be recognised here, on the basis of its being a judgment.[10] From a practical aspect, it will be realised that any other attitude towards the collection here of assets by a foreign liquidator is going to be difficult to maintain. It is in this sphere that one may see that "jurisdiction" is essentially a matter of fact. The policy of mutual tolerance towards the jurisdiction of another country is justifiable as an inroad upon national sovereignty. The relaxation of this sovereignty stems from the concept of reciprocity. An English court can hardly refuse rights to residents, corporate or otherwise, of foreign countries if English law pre-supposes that, when the position of the parties is reversed, British residents are going to be given by foreign courts the very rights that the English court is being asked to concede to the foreign applicant.

Before dealing with foreign companies and the practical banking side of our subject it is well to be helpful to explain two definitions: oversea company and unregistered company. Both are contained in the Companies Act 1985 and both are relevant to foreign businesses

---

[8] *Vide infra.*
[9] Income Tax Act 1952, s.468(7).
[10] The authority of the foreign liquidator has been recognised here. See the cases quoted in Dicey, Conflict of Laws (10th ed.), n. 37. A willingness to regard a German bankruptcy as a judgment enforceable in the United Kingdom can be seen in the recent case of *Berliner Industrie bank, A.G.* v. *Jost* [1971] 2 Q.B. 463.

that may have liabilities and/or assets here. An *oversea company* by section 744 of the Companies Act 1985 is one that is incorporated outside Great Britain and that has established a place of business within Great Britain. As a consequence its constitution has to be on record with the Registrar of Companies, with a translation in English. In addition such companies are required to register particulars of officials and a person authorised to accept service of legal proceedings. Of more interest, any company incorporated outside Great Britain that carries on business here and is therefore an "oversea company" has to register charges on property of any kind in Great Britain that would have required registration if the company had been an English company.[11] This latter requirement has seldom been before the courts. One wonders whether it would extend to property situate outside Great Britain but which may come within the ambit of a floating charge given here. Probably it would do so because the undertaking of the company, which is subject to the floating charge, would be regarded as being in its entirety within the jurisdiction. An *"unregistered company"* however includes *inter alia* "any partnership, whether limited or not, any association and any company"[12] except of course a *registered United Kingdom company* or limited partnership, and, incidentally, railway companies. There is a further exclusion where the unregistered body has less than eight members, *but* this further exclusion does *not* apply to any foreign partnership, association or company. It is also helpful to bear in mind the difference between winding-up and dissolution. In broad terms winding-up is the process involving the collection of assets and payment of dividends whereas dissolution is the legal termination of the company's life. Normally the first precedes the second although there is now specific statutory provision[13] for the winding-up notwithstanding the earlier dissolution of the company.

An English court has not only the power to wind-up an English company but also by section 664 of the Companies Act 1985 it has power to wind-up an unregistered company. Within this category are "oversea" companies which are not only incorporated abroad but do business here, as well as other foreign companies of all types, foreign associations and partnerships. There are a number of grounds upon which such a petition will be granted[14]: if the company has been dissolved by the courts of the country where it was incorporated or has ceased to carry on business; or is so doing only for the purpose of being wound-up; if it cannot pay its debts; or, it is considered by the court "just and equitable" that it be wound-up (this latter includes as with English companies such matters as an

---

[11] Companies Act 1985, s.691 *et. seq.*
[12] *Idem*, section 665.
[13] *Idem*, section 666(5).
[14] *Idem*, section 666.

impasse among directors or where one director takes an inequitable advantage of his position). The decision whether to grant the petition is (again as with an English company) in the discretion of the court. If, *e.g.* the company is already being wound-up abroad the petition may be refused. Where a liquidation is taking place, *e.g.* in Australia[15] and there is a fair opportunity for English creditors to participate the court would be likely to be unwilling for them to obtain advantage by liquidation here. A more modern case was that of in *re N. V. Handelmaatschappij Wokar* [1946] Ch. 98; the company was being liquidated in Holland where it was incorporated but, following service at the address in London where its main business had been previously carried on, the English petition was granted. There had been failure to register at the Companies Registry such particulars as were then required. Moreover it will be noted that there is no need to have a place of business here. If there are English creditors and available assets a winding-up order may be obtained.[16]

THE BANKER CREDITOR

The primary purpose for our dissertation is not to examine the law but to suggest to the banker. Let us assume that there is an unsecured debt or a claim by reason of the banker having given a guarantee on behalf of a customer. The customer has gone abroad leaving no evidence of his destination, or is a limited company and appears to have "evaporated" with even less trace than the human customer; or, again, you may know of insolvency proceedings or the activity of execution creditors against a customer. What can be done with advantage? As with domestic banking, without knowledge, belief or hope as to the existence of assets any pursuit is likely to give no material satisfaction. It may lead to exposure and possibly criminal proceedings; at all events many bankruptcy offences are not extraditable. It may give future protection to yourselves or to others. This however is likely to be only temporary because in international business there is greater scope for the anonymity beloved of the criminal mind than within a national territory. Remotely a personal customer, or perhaps his relatives, may be sensitive to bankruptcy, especially within particular national boundaries. On the other hand, if they are faced with demands for substantial sums of money, they seem to become inured to vicarious disrepute, that sometimes has resulted from misfortune and, if not, is easily accepted by others as having done so.

As to the possibilities: with the individual, if he is made bankrupt in England, the Order may be enforced in Scotland and Northern

---

[15] *Re Commercial Bank of South Australia* (1886) 33 Ch.D. 174.
[16] *Re Azoff-Don Commercial Bank* [1954] Ch. 315.

Ireland.[17] In Eire there is a system of Orders in Aid. The courts of some foreign countries will recognise the claims of an English trustee on the principle of the recognition of an assignment. This method of pursuit is satisfactory only if the assets are enough to pay a substantial dividend. Sometimes bankruptcy proceedings abroad will prevent foreign creditors from seizing assets but this is a worthwhile thought only if the amount is large and the advice from a local lawyer is positive.

If a banker is an unsecured creditor and is not reasonably confident of the existence of sufficient assets he himself may wish to try to obtain priority by attachment. When he has obtained judgment this remedy is well established here. As to assets abroad a money judgment may be registered as a local judgment in most Commonwealth or Colonial countries as well as in some parts of Europe. The prospect of execution will depend on the law and the assets in the foreign country. It is often a lengthy process. The practical difficulty is always that assets abroad are almost always more difficult to trace than assets here. Frequently the amount concerned will not justify the expense of foreign proceedings. It is worth recalling, however, that an English creditor may obtain an advantage by seeking execution against English assets, despite a foreign bankruptcy having commenced.[18] An English trustee in bankruptcy is able, of course, to require the debtor to do all that may be necessary even in respect of foreign land.[19] Thus, to summarise, if he knows of no assets upon which he has a prospect of attachment here or, perhaps exceptionally abroad, the creditor may move for bankruptcy in England. There may be circumstances that encourage initiating bankruptcy abroad but, as with any attempt to seize assets outside the jurisdiction, the disadvantages of an English creditor pursuing insolvency proceedings abroad may often be technical consequent upon his being a non-resident or an alien in the eyes of the foreign law and the foreign courts; of sometimes more disconcerting embarrassment there is his own unfamiliarity with what is going on, added to the feeling on some occasions, in relation to more remote areas, that he is not "one of them." This latter sentiment, with the English-speaking countries and to a large degree with Europe is ebbing; but in practice the factor may deter the pursuit that otherwise might have been attempted. At times one may connect it with a certain inconcrete and procrastinating attitude towards business that inevitably

---

[17] Bankruptcy Act 1914, s.121. This section was repealed by the Insolvency Act 1985, Sched. 10, Pt. IV. See n. 40.

[18] *Galbraith* v. *Grimshaw* [1910] A.C. 508 (although see also, possibly to the contrary the much earlier case of *Solomons* v. *Ross* (1764) 1 Hy. Bl. 131.

[19] Bankruptcy Act 1914, s.22. This section was repealed by the Insolvency Act 1985, Sched. 10, Pt. III. See n. 40. See also *Selkrigg* v. *Davies* (1814) 2 Rose, 97.

pervades the courts. The attitude may at times appear to be associated with proximity to the Equator; yet it appears also occasionally much nearer home, where a nation has, perhaps in a way to its credit much less cynicism about the "fey" and the "folklore" than the English.

INACTIVE COMPANIES

With the derelict limited company customer incorporated here, liquidation will usually be the better method of collecting assets abroad. Of course, if by chance a banker holds a floating charge then the receiver he appoints will probably be able to achieve as much as a liquidator. Nevertheless whilst, like a liquidator, he can use the seal and can force English directors to co-operate, the winding-up process may have the same effect abroad as an English judgment, which would not necessarily be the case with a crystallised floating charge. Therefore the English creditor may obtain advantage by liquidation, especially if there does not appear to be an inordinate measure of conflict of interest between the bankers as holders of the floating charge and the general body of creditors.

If the company is incorporated abroad and has assets here a winding-up involving distribution of the English assets to English creditors is likely to be an advantage. This course can be followed whether or not the company has been carrying on business here and whether or not it is registered as an oversea company.[20] In the latter event its constitution will be known, but the extent to which its assets have been charged will be evident only in so far as they are in this country and come within the categories requiring registration by an English company. The extent to which the status of an English liquidator will be recognised and to which the courts here will recognise a liquidator appointed in the place of incorporation is sometimes of practical interest. Primarily he can act on behalf of the corporation.[21] In the Russian Bank cases,[22] which turned principally on whether there had been only a winding-up or also a dissolution it was implied that a foreign liquidator would not be given any further recognition and could not set up title to the company's property, moveable or immoveable, in this country. The position is also bedevilled by the technical aspect that in some foreign countries there is one term, "bankruptcy," applied to companies as well as individuals and also that in some countries the appointment of a liquidator may purport to be an assignment of assets in all countries.

---

[20] Companies Act, 1985, ss.665 *et. seq. Re Azoff–Don Commercial Bank* [1954] Ch. 315
[21] Cp. *Banco de Bilbao* [11938] 2 K.B. 176.
[22] See, *e.g. Russian Commercial and Industrial Bank* v. *Comptoir d'Escompte de Mulhouse* [1925] A.C. 112.

It is on this basis that a measure of recognition and title is given here to a foreign official, in whom his local law has vested all property by way of assignment.[23] If there is an English liquidator he can, of course, give a good discharge to a banker having a credit balance. Whether a foreign liquidator can given an English banker a good discharge for such monies is open to doubt and for this reason it may be wise when large sums are involved to seek an order of an English court, despite the possibility that the banker could be mulcted for the costs. Contrariwise, however, there is no doubt that there may be advantage to an English creditor in petitioning for the company to be wound-up here as an "unregistered" company. These provisions are wide and extend to any group of any number of persons who are associated together by way of business and have assets here. This is helpful where there are foreign domiciled bodies that have done business here and it is not quite clear whether they are regarded by their local law as being separate entities.

PRIORITIES

Within this description it is intended to include not only the implications of security or attachment but the material consequences of bankruptcy. Obviously all creditors will endeavour to minimise their losses by realising their security to the maximum advantage, by seeking to obtain satisfaction of a judgment in priority to other creditors and by proving wherever possible. Perhaps even a similar end may be achieved, *vis-à-vis* a foreign bankruptcy in which a debtor may have to account in the absence of an English bankruptcy, by a creditor taking, on terms coupled with an indemnity, an assignment from another creditor. Set-off is a difficult enough problem in English bankruptcy and the complications (and perhaps the morality) of its application in a foreign bankruptcy are speculative. Such a device would be dependent upon the vulnerability of the English debtor and the effect of assignments at particular times in accordance with the rules of the foreign bankruptcy. Because of his vulnerability to actions abroad the last mentioned exercise is unlikely to be of attraction to a banker, quite apart perhaps from ethical considerations. However, it illustrates the perplexity of the subject in practice.

One has to appreciate that the method of distribution will vary. In Scotland a banker finds it harder to avoid a claim of fraudulent preference[24] than in an English bankruptcy, although for Scotland and Northern Ireland the bankruptcy jurisdiction is one with England in

---

[23] See *Macaulay* v. *Guaranty Trust Co. of New York* (1927) 44 T.L.R. 99, which indicates treatment of claimant on basis of bankruptcy.

[24] In England a dominant intention to prefer has to be established; the burden is not so great in Scotland.

that the title of the trustee is recognised in all the three countries. The claim of a foreign trustee or administrator, if earlier than an English bankruptcy, will be recognised in respect of assets in England if his appointment covers assets anywhere.[25] If, however, as in some states[26] it purports to deal only with assets within the State the trustee will not be able to claim English assets despite the bankruptcy being earlier than any English bankruptcy. There is an exception relating to immoveable property in England in respect of which a foreign bankruptcy purporting to create a universal assignment is not recognised[27] (although a receiver has been on occasions appointed to collect the rents on behalf of the foreign trustee).[28] A Dutch trustee has even been allowed to claim a debt due to the Dutch bankruptcy despite an English creditor having commenced attachment, although some decisions have permitted the attachment to be completed.[29] Where there has been a bankruptcy by the law of the domicile of a foreign debtor then a court here will refuse to grant a bankruptcy petition if in fact there are no assets here.[30] Often there may be assets that are not available to the foreign trustee because he cannot claim title by "relation back" as can an English trustee or because there is land here for which a foreign trustee is not recognised.

Where the debtor is a company incorporated abroad the same question arises as to whether the proceedings, which may be called bankruptcy proceedings and operate like them, purport to be a prior assignment and to have effect beyond the territory. (If that is so it is possible that it will be permitted to take precedence over a winding-up in this country.)[31]

For practical bankers the problems of priorities are only too evident but in some senses the steps to take are simple. One cannot help having the impression that contrary to the Proverbs "the race *is* to the swift." One does not wish to disturb one's customers and bring trouble here when it might perhaps be avoided. Otherwise, as soon as insolvency proceedings are undertaken abroad, whether your personal customer is domiciled here or in the foreign country and whether your impersonal customer is an English registered company or is an unregistered company, the presentation of a petition in England, or an attempt to satisfy an English judgment from English assets is to be pursued expeditiously. Of course this is assuming that you are confident that you will not be repaid from

---

[25] *Re Anderson* [1911] 1 K.B. 896.
[26] *Cf.* Dicey, Conflict of Laws (10th ed.) p. 220.
[27] *Cockerell* v. *Dickens* (1840), 3 Moo. P.C. 98.
[28] *Re Kooperman* (1928), 13 B. & C.R. 49. (*Hansell's Bankruptcy Reports*).
[29] *Solomon* v. *Ross* (1764) 1 H.Bl. 131) and *Galbraith* v. *Grimshaw* [1910] A.C. 508.
[30] *Ex p. Robinson* (1883), 22 Ch.D. 816.
[31] This is upon the analogy of the bankruptcy cases of *Re Blithman* 35 Beav. 219; *Re Anderson* (supra) and *Re Craig* (1916) 86 L.J. Ch. 62.

security and, alternatively, that your customer will not in any case weather the storm. For validity of your security taken *here* is of course ascertained in the normal way whatever the rules of any foreign bankruptcy. It will sometimes be that there are insolvency administrations, either bankruptcy or company liquidation of an international institution, such as a foreign bank, in two or three different jurisdictions.[32] Then there is an element of chance as to proving. If at the time of proving in the English proceedings a dividend has been received from a foreign bankruptcy the amount has to be brought into account. On the other hand, this is not the case if the dividend has not been received from abroad.[33] Yet before a further dividend is received from the English distribution any foreign dividend actually received must be allowed by way of offset. Occasionally trustees may agree to act on a "pooling" basis, which an English court is likely to support.[34] In practice there are so many competing interests, whose advisers think that they can obtain an advantage, or in fact perhaps have already done so, that the prospects of a compromise are poor. The spirit of self-sacrifice can hardly be expected even to flicker among creditors of an insolvent debtor; in fact the main attraction towards a compromise is the avoidance of costly litigation and ancillary administration expenses.

Inevitably the banker will wonder whether a foreigner who is made bankrupt abroad gets a good discharge from his English debt, or if he, say, comes to England later and there has been no English bankruptcy, whether he can be pursued through the courts in the ordinary way. If the contract from which the debt arose was itself subject to the law of the country where the bankruptcy took place, then the debt is discharged here.[35] If the nature of the discharge does not have the effect of extinguishing the debt but merely preventing an action being brought then there will be no question of the debtor being discharged in respect of his English debt.[36] Thus if it is thought that there is a future prospect of the debtor acquiring assets following upon his foreign bankruptcy and that either he would come here or in some way, perhaps by enforcement of an English judgment abroad, become vulnerable to the English courts, then and then only will inactivity benefit the creditor. This is probably a course few bankers would be willing to speculate upon. Clearly there may also be problems if an English banker is faced with a customer who is an undischarged bankrupt from a jurisdiction where the effect of the foreign court is recognised as an assignment. Presum-

---

[32] *Levasseur* v. *Mason and Barry Ltd.* (1891), 2 Q.B. 73, where creditors who had benefited from an English distribution by a receiver of certain assets appointed to satisfy a judgment were allowed also to prove in a French liquidation.
[33] *Cf.* Dicey, Conflict of Laws (10th ed.) p. 665.
[34] In *Re Macfadyen & Co. (No. 1)* (1880), 14 Ch.D. 716.
[35] *Ellis* v. *McHenry* (1871, L.R. 6 C.P. 228).
[36] *Gibbs* v. *Société Industrielle des Métaux* (1890) 25 Q.B.D. 399.

ably dealing with assets such as the collecting of a cheque to which the customer would otherwise be entitled may be a conversion and, if the banker knows the background he would be deemed to have been sufficiently negligent to lose his protection under section 4 of the Cheques Act, quite apart from other dealings for which he has no protection to lose. This subject of insolvency is among the most difficult and summary is more than ever necessary. The most significant conclusions are:

(1) If the banker feels at risk he should initiate all remedies in this country as soon as possible, including attachment of any assets after having obtained a judgment. This will be desirable if the debtor is abroad or is a company registered abroad. The banker need not, however, be concerned in any way as to the realisation of any security that he may hold in the United Kingdom.
(2) In all insolvencies there can be no disadvantage in proving in all the distributions.
(3) Any insolvent company, whether registered here or not, may be wound-up by an English court. If there are English assets and unsatisfied English creditors a winding-up Order will be granted irrespective of whether the company in existence abroad is in fact a company or any other form of association.
(4) A foreign liquidator will be recognised here as an agent of the company. Whether or not he can give a good discharge for assets is not certain.
(5) A discharge under a foreign bankruptcy is effective only if the contract from which the debt arises is governed by the law of the foreign country whose courts have granted the discharge.

GUARANTEES AND INDEMNITIES ON BEHALF OF CUSTOMERS

It is obvious that a banker's guarantee is an attractive feature of international commerce. The contingent undertaking has the attraction that it may never materialise. In some ways it has similarities with a letter of credit, in that the credit-worthiness of the banker is interposed into the commercial transaction. On the other hand in a letter of credit the banker is under a primary obligation in contradistinction to a guarantee which is secondary, in that it arises only if the principal debtor or obligor fails to meet his liability.[37] From a financial standpoint bankers have decided to limit, especially in domestic transactions, the extent to which they are willing to become guarantors. As a matter of general principle they will not guarantee trade debts. But for this decision one can envisage a very large proportion of the ordinary credit given to by traders to traders being backed by

---

[37] See Gutteridge and Megrah, *Law of Bankers Commercial Credits* (7th ed.), at p. 52.

banks. To customers the method would prove more attractive than having an overdraft; but for bankers it would create a super-structure of impeccable credit the extent and entanglement of which it would be impossible to evaluate or unravel. We are not concerned here with the types of guarantee that banks will give, domestically or internationally. As with all extra-legal matters definition rather than administration has proved difficult, in that the compass of the restrictions has been frequently refined by a number of ad hoc decisions. At all events the policy does not obtrude so largely into foreign transactions.

With all guarantees given by bankers there is one general policy aspect that has to be the keystone: that is that the banker is *not* the arbiter of the contract but is essentially the financial backer. If this were not so his involvement would be overwhelming. Our practical purpose is to ascertain the legal problems involved for bankers in entering into these undertakings and consider ways in which those problems can be minimised or, if possible, eliminated.

The counter indemnity

Many of the foreign banker's legal problems can be exorcised of their devilment if formal approval is obtained from the customer on whose behalf the banker is acting. This does not mean that the benefit of the banker's experience is not to be forthcoming. It is not however for the banker to take over the disputes and the risks involved in their resolution; the banker has taken his risk when he decided to warrant his customer's creditworthiness. It is upon these basic principles that the customer will be asked to give the banker a counter-indemnity. Essentially, this relates specifically to the main guarantee being given, which can be more satisfactorily indicated by the attachment of an initialled copy than by the most precise description. By the terms of the counter-indemnity the banker is authorised to give the guarantee against the assurance from the customer as to reimbursement of all that the banker may thereby incur by way of claims costs and damages. Because the main obligation will often be governed explicitly or implicitly by the law of a foreign country and perhaps also be referable solely to the courts of that country, it is wise for the counter-indemnity to be made specifically subject to English law. There can then be no doubt that the turns and twists that may emerge from moratoria, exchange variations, expropriations and other creatures of foreign governments do not diminish or postpone the rights of the banker to be reimbursed by his customer.

Again the counter-indemnity will usually authorise the banker to pay upon demand being made by the beneficiary of the guarantee.[38]

---

[38] As to demand it is of interest to see the desirability of evidencing the "demand" as suggested in the case of *Esal (Commodities)* v. *Oriental Credit* [1985] 2 Lloyd's Rep. 546, C.A.

This clause, although commonplace, is one that may sometimes give rise to difficulty. The customer will be hesitant, because he senses a loss of control, augmented perhaps by his consciousness of the physical remoteness. He must nevertheless appreciate that the banker is vulnerable at the instance of the beneficiary of the guarantee as to his assets, and also as to his goodwill, in a foreign jurisdiction where, in the ultimate he cannot ignore a judgment however unorthodox its law and its justice. These are factors implicit in the risk of trading with a particular country and reflected in the estimated profit. This problem is discussed separately a little later in this volume in that it is among the most difficult and that practical steps taken may depend on the particular circumstances. It is on the other hand fundamentally important for the banker to be authorised in the counter-indemnity to meet the first demand. If the customer at the outset suspects the beneficiary of the guarantee as being unscrupulous, the contingency can hardly be passed to the banker as the "fall guy." However, in practice, the answer is as to many legal complications, that the *system works*. The counter-indemnity will also contain for the sake of clarity an authority to debit the customer's account with whatever may be paid. This had the advantage that upon implementation of an undertaking given on behalf of a customer there is a reimbursement rather than a right to hold a balance by way of lien or set-off (whichever term one may chose to use).[39] It may result in an addition to an overdraft but in any event the legal position of the banker is clearer.

The term *"counter"* indemnity has been used, but the wording will obviously have to be varied where a guarantee has to be given to the banker himself, acting in "another capacity." He cannot conveniently sue himself, and the description of the liability must be different.

The type of guarantee

The intrinsic variations in guarantees are as extensive as the complexities of the underlying commercial transactions. Yet the obligations undertaken fall into categories. These are: undertakings for repayment of advance payments contingent upon failure of the customer to perform the contract; undertakings, sometimes given as bonds under seal, for the performance of the contract as a whole;

---

[39] Strictly, probably set-off because it is a credit balance that is being held against a monetary claim. This largely academic subject is ventilated in the case of *Halesowen Presswork & Assemblies Ltd.* v. *Westminster Bank Ltd.* [1971] 1 Q.B. 1; where the Master of the Rolls extends controversially the term "set off" to include the banker's right to a cheque received for collection—despite presumably the fact that it may be returned to him dishonoured by non-payment.

bail bonds to obtain the release of ships held after collisions or seized abroad as cover against claims by local nationals; to a limited extent, undertakings relating to reimbursement of import deposits; indemnities regarding irregularities in documentary credits; again to a very limited extent, there are guarantees involving the future payment of money by customers; tender bonds also frequently offer the acceptance of a banker's guarantee as an alternative to a cash deposit. In the latter connection it may be salutary to warn the less experienced customer of the possibility that the terms of the tender may involve a commitment, indefinite in point of time, pending the acceptance or rejection of rival tenders. This can be protracted because the existence of competing tenders, also *supported by tender bonds,* may be a factor enabling the prospective "employer" to exact better terms from the selected tenderer.

Another type of guarantee, becoming increasingly popular with the multiplication of customer's subsidiaries and associates abroad, is the guarantee of a facility made available by a foreign banker. Usually this is a short term loan or credit, but sometimes it may be a revolving facility or even a longer term commitment, always so much the feature of European banking and for sometime past a growing and somewhat esoteric factor in the United Kingdom. Either explicitly or implicitly these guarantees between bankers are almost invariably payable on first demand.

Often a banker will be asked to draft a guarantee. Then there must be an understanding that the responsibility for the wording devolves on the customer, who may of course consult their own legal advisers, it being remembered that the banker has usually not seen the contract. This choice of one of several standard forms is just part of general expedition that may be required. Obviously it is vital that the customers shall approve the wording adopted. Again, there may be a standard form required by the prospective beneficiary; frequently it is an appendix of the main export contract. Even more are the customers in the hands of the parties with whom they are contracting abroad, when a guarantee is required as a matter of great urgency; then the United Kingdom banker, and basically the United Kingdom customer, will authorise a guarantee to be given by the banking correspondent abroad in the terms required subject to limitations of time and amount.

The essential features

Practical considerations will cause bankers to ignore many of the infelicities of drafting in the documents they are asked to give or in which they are asked to join on behalf of customers. Many will have stemmed from difficulties of translation. (Legal terms of other nations have no true translation). On the other hand there are two essential features with which the banker must be concerned: these are the inclusion either expressly or, beyond all doubt impliedly, of an overall maximum liability and secondly the certainty as to the occasion of payment. In relation to the first-mentioned stipulation it is important to indicate the currency. If the liability is to be in sterling, then in view of possible doubts it is worth indicating that the liability can be discharged in sterling in London.[40] If there is a currency liability then it may be desirable to indicate in the counter-indemnity the method of ascertaining the rate of conversion. Probably the scope of the counter-indemnity would mean in any event complete restitution for the banker, but the point also merits attention in relation specifically to any maximum inserted. With regard to the occasion of payment, this means the evidence that is to be produced to the banker as an indication that he has to pay. An ideal is an authority signed by both parties to the contract involved, with an arbitration or court order by way of alternative; in the latter event it will be well to indicate that the court order should be that of an English court unless, as may sometimes be, the contract is subject to the courts of a foreign country, in which event there should be a reference in the guarantee to an order from the foreign court. Often the parties will not be willing to be so dependent on each other's good sense. Then the banker may have to envisage just how clear and unambiguous is the evidence likely to be offered. If he thinks he is insulated from becoming involved in the interpretation of the contract he will take what is offered; otherwise he will demur.

When claims are made

At the outset it may be helpful to deal with claims under guarantees stipulating for payment on first demand, including those guarantees given by one banker to another in which such undertaking may, generally speaking, be regarded as customary in the absence of indications to the contrary. Although such a guarantee had not been before an English court the point was litigated in Israel.[41] A guarantee payable on first demand had been given in relation to a liability under a lease but demand was made in relation to a liability under a loan. Nevertheless payment had to be made. When evidence is not clear and a dispute exists it is necessary for the banker to consider a number of alternatives all of which may have merit according to the circumstances. One course is to give one's own customer 24 hours (or perhaps 48) in which to apply to court for an injunction to prevent payment. However, this is likely to be successful only when forgery or fraud is established. It is of no avail that one of the parties is

---

[40] One can pay sterling in notes abroad.
[41] 1 C.A. 298/63 17 P.D. 2814 reported in The Banker's Magazine, October 1970. See also *The Brimnes* [1975] Q.B. 929 and Paget, *Law of Banking* (10th ed.), p. 567.

merely in breach of contract.[42] A second method is to pay the money to a joint account. Thirdly, the bank might open an account on deposit for a fixed period for the claimant. These are half measures but they buy time and in the event of there being a genuine dispute sometimes satisfy the parties concerned. Where a guarantee has been given by a banker abroad on behalf of a London bank it has to be realised that that banker may be obliged to pay over immediately. The guarantee that he has given will be subject to his local law which may mean that immediate payment cannot be gainsaid. In practice the difficulties are sometimes less than may be expected because the parties either are conscious of their common interest in future business, or because the claimant knows that if he commences proceedings under the basic contract and is successful the money will be available to satisfy such order as the court may make.

Summary

The practical aspects of importance are:

(1) a clear counter indemnity subject to English law;
(2) a maximum liability in the principal guarantee;
(3) a clear indication as to the evidence to be produced before payment may be demanded;
(4) in relation to claims emphasis that the banker's function is as financial backer and *not* as arbiter of the contract.

Documentary credits

Both the law and the practical problems arising for the banker have been ventilated previously and the inclusion of this reference is merely a reminder that this facet is *one* source, one of the main sources, of legal problems involving foreign banking. In relation to the legal background on which the book is based, jurisdiction and conflict of law, there are two situations to which attention may be profitably drawn.

The indemnity

Indirectly the indemnity that is given when documents tendered under a letter of credit fail to conform with its requirements may concern the question of jurisdiction or of conflict of laws. It is also a matter of considerable practical importance. There is no doubt that the indemnity given to a banker, whether he is paying or negotiating a draft will have served in a very large majority of cases to avoid fric-

---

[42] This may be seen from the case of *British Imex Industries Ltd.* v. *Midland Bank Ltd.* [1958] 1 Q.B. 542 (later confirmed on appeal) where it was made clear that the bank could not refuse payment in the absence of evidence of forgery or fraud. This case related to a documentary credit, but the principle would be likely to be applied in the case of a guarantee.

tion and delay. The indemnity can cover one or more different types of reason for the banker refusing to pay or negotiate: some documents may have been omitted; or those included may not accord with the terms and conditions of the credit; or, the documents in themselves may be out of order, such as a bill of lading being claused. Then an indemnity alluding to the defect will normally be taken from the presenting party or his banker. This will probably simply refer to the nature of the defect and indicate that the *paying banker* is indemnified.

The meaning of the indemnity

The intention of the paying bankers is that as soon as the documents reach the recipient, that is the buyer or the buyer's banker, he is obliged to pay or return the documents almost immediately upon their receipt. At all events to keep them without objection might amount to ratification irrespective of whether the recipient's attention has been drawn to the defect or not.[43] Thus the contention and, with respect, the better view is that the recipient (or principal) has no interest in the indemnity received by the bank paying or negotiating the credit. He either keeps the documents and the matter ends; or, he rejects them and is reimbursed by the banker who in turn is reimbursed by the party to whom he made payment under an indemnity. This is how indemnities should and for the most part do operate.

Another possibility

Dependent very much upon the wording of the indemnity there is another view that is sometimes advanced. This is that the party to whom the banker passes the documents has an option to take the documents with the benefit of the indemnity. Of course, if the wording of the indemnity makes it clear that the documents have to be rejected promptly, if they are going to be rejected, or accepted *in the form in which they were tendered* then the possibility cannot arise. In practice this admonition is frequently contained with varying degrees of emphasis in a covering letter. There again the matter ends. However, in the absence of language either in the covering letter or the indemnity, placing the point beyond doubt, suggestions arise as to the intention of the parties. There are some aspects that may encourage the view that the recipient of the documents can take the benefit of the indemnity if he retains them. Whilst the intention may be to reimburse the paying banker only, there is no reason why the benefit of such an indemnity should not be assigned, if by its terms, such a possibility is not precluded specifically. No formal

---

[43] Gutteridge & Megrah, *The Law of Commercial Credits* (7th ed.), p. 192 *et. seq.*

words are necessary.[44] In fact the covering letter itself could well provide, unintentionally perhaps, the modicum of evidence sufficient for the recipient of the document to make out his case as an assignee. If, for example an indemnity is in general terms, indemnifying the banker from any consequence arising from the particular defect and the covering letter, say to the buyer's banker in Holland, indicates the defect mentioning "but we hold an indemnity" or that "the documents have been tendered with an indemnity," sending a copy of the indemnity itself, there are the seeds of an equitable assignment. An alternative view, to the same effect, is that the banker has acknowledged that he holds it as agent of the buyer's banker. There is another possible legal argument that might be used to support the contention: the period usually inserted of six months (the legal effect of which is sometimes controversial) may be suggested as being quite inconsistent with the obligation to "take or leave" the documents. Occasionally this misconception may find substance in what is probably imprecise language in law reports or judgments. For example, in the case of *Soproma S.p.A.* v. *Marine and Animal By-Products Corporation*[45] there is a reference in the head-note to the "buyers declining to accept the guarantee."[46] Later in the summary of the facts[47] it is mentioned that the "buyers refused to accept the guarantee." In the judgment[48] McNair J., refers to the bankers having "accepted the letter of guarantee by the sellers as sufficient evidence that the freight had been paid." It is true that as a finding the judgment is that[49] the bankers had not "waived any rights of the buyers in forwarding the documents first tendered after taking a letter of guarantee" and that they could not have done so. However, at worst, it is clearly wise to eliminate the possibility of misunderstanding. Reverting to the example of the despatch of documents to Holland it has to be appreciated that if the Dutch banker is sued by his customer, the buyer, because the documents received are irregular the measure of damage will be decided in Holland according to Dutch law. Thus problems of jurisdiction and of conflict of laws make the need for indemnities taken in respect of documentary credit irregularities *and for any letters accompanying the despatch of the relevant documents* to have no semblance of ambiguity; otherwise there is the possibility, that has occasionally occurred in practice, of dispute as to the availability of the indemnity.[50]

Of course, the wide adoption of the Uniform Customs does much

---

[44] See *Law of Contract Cheshire & Fifoot* (8th ed.), Part VI, Chap. 3.
[45] (1966) 1 Lloyd's Rep. 367.
[46] *Ibid.* p. 367.
[47] *Ibid* p. 367.
[48] *Ibid* p. 379 *et seq.*
[49] (1966) 1 Lloyds Reports 390.
[50] It is however, to be noted, that an opinion by the Banking Technique Commission, relating to payment subject to reserve, militates against the possibility.

to reduce the number of problems of conflict of laws that might otherwise arise. Where there is a large measure of common provisions there is much less upon which the laws of the respective countries may conflict. Nevertheless, there are two clear sources by which problems of conflict of laws can intrude; first, it is apparent that courts of different countries may construe the Uniform Customs differently, an aspect upon which no doubt records will be kept by the office of the International Chamber of Commerce with a view to future clarification; the second is the more elusive differential produced by the application of other sections of the law of a particular country. An example is to be found in the facts of an unreported case litigated in Switzerland where, following the failure to return irregular documents prompted by the practical consequences of damage to the cargo through non-acceptance on arrival, judgment was given against a Swiss bank. If the case had been heard in England and English law had been applied the principle of the quasi-authority of an "agent of necessity" may have caused a different decision to have been reached. Sometimes foreign law may determine the effect of a particular document, but the modern principle of applying were possible the law of the country with which the transaction has the closest connection[51] is likely to be followed, as in the *Soproma* case[52] where, despite the bill of lading being subject to Italian law, the court considered that its transferability would not be thereby affected, since the contract of sale was governed by English law.

As mentioned previously only oblique references have been made to the subject of documentary credits merely to show that, although the Uniform Customs have done much to eliminate the impact of "jurisdiction" and "conflict of laws," these difficult facets still may occasionally obtrude. To some extent the Uniform Customs permit this in their acknowledgment that local usage may affect the question as to whether or not a particular document is good tender.

The only aspect meriting summary is the need for maximum care in the wording of an indemnity for irregular documents so that it is clear that the documents have either to be rejected or accepted; and, also, the letter accompanying the documents must not in any way detract from this understanding.

THE BANKER AS BAILEE AND AS AGENT

The only justification for this arbitrary division is that the function of bailee, the custody and redelivery of items, is often coupled with an additional obligation devolving on the banker, which further function he performs as an agent. He may also be asked to do some-

---

[51] See p. 8.
[52] *Ubi supra* at p. 367.

thing as an agent in which there is no question of his also being a bailee. He may be asked as an agent to make payments which he does on instructions (sometimes on standing instructions). It may then be suggested that he is merely a paying agent. An example would be when he has to pay bond interest coupon to holders or in which he is instructed to cable money or send a bankers draft to a third party.

In all these cases including safe custody work his obligations will be determined by English law. Any action brought against him is generally speaking likely to be brought in England, and, even if this is not so, a foreign court will usually apply English law.

Whilst more often than not the banker's principal will be another banker, there will sometimes be instructions direct from a customer who has a foreign domicile, is a foreign national, or is a foreign registered company. If the banker in the United Kingdom needs to sue such a principal he will then have to consider not only the prospects of English law being applied by the foreign court, if it differs from the local law, but also the extent to which any judgment obtained may be satisfied. The enforcement of a judgment obtained in a foreign country may be difficult and, with regard to the more simple methods of enforcement of a foreign judgment here, such as by registration, it has to be remembered that the procedure is limited to a money judgment. It could not be applied, *e.g.* to an order of a foreign court requiring the despatch of securities from England. If damages *in lieu* were ordered it would be a different matter. Fundamentally one can see on reflection that the performance of the one is difficult to ordain whereas, given assets within the jurisdiction, the enforcement of the money judgment is feasible. Thus, as bailee and as agent the need to litigate abroad will be rare; the wisdom of doing so will be even rarer.

It is relevant to mention that an English banker as bailee may be concerned, as in fact he is as agent and as banker, with instructions that appear to flout the exchange control of another country. This aspect is examined in the next chapter when considering exchange control. Similarly, a cleft-stick situation arises if assets held on behalf of a foreign sovereign are subjected to a third party claim. The normal course of interpleading is no longer available. However usually the foreign party having immunity will agree to appear.

One problem may arise in relation to agency work. A third party here may attempt to give notice to an English banker of his claim, perhaps a good claim, as an assignee of monies that in the future may well be paid to the banker. Just as if its receipt were contemplated by a domestic banker, the agent banker here who may at sometime in the future receive, say, payment from a foreign banker, perhaps a central exchange bank making payments when sufficient currency is available, cannot be saddled with an obligation to the assignee unless he agrees. It is submitted that this view appears to be justified by the case of *Williams* v. *Everett*[53] where a claim was made upon an agent banker before proceeds of a bill were received and the recipient held not liable to the claimant. A contrary decision would make domestic banking impracticable and there is no legal or practical justification for taking a different view because the principal is abroad.

There is however one instance when the banker will have to measure carefully the prospects of litigation. He may pay abroad by mistake as to destination or amount (or for that matter misdeliver a security), in circumstances in which recovery would be possible here. An action can be brought here notwithstanding the absence abroad of the defendant[54] but the problem of satisfaction of a judgment will arise. Individuals or companies abroad may for tax or other reasons have their assets in a third country. Indiviuals may be nationals of, or companies may be registered in, a fourth country. In practice the recovery abroad of mistaken payments is very often a difficult problem without the intervention of an agent banker whose displeasure often seems to be a more powerful factor than legal liability to an English banker. This is perhaps as it should be. It may also be true in reverse.[55]

As a summary of a banker as a bailee and an agent it may be truly said that the problems of jurisdiction and conflict of laws are likely to concern him but little more than they do as paying banker.

SECRECY

This obligation, and the difficulties it may bring on the question of jurisdiction, is largely limited to institutions with branches abroad. Examples of the difficulties were noticed in the first chapter.[56] Each case depends on its particular circumstances. Although evidence here can be obtained by the courts of many countries on a reciprocal arrangement the system is ponderous involving question and answer on oath. Where a witness cannot be persuaded to attend in person the problems for the litigants are sometimes so important and so difficult to elucidate that the enquirer has been known to initiate proceedings on a remote pretext because more information can be obtained from a litigant by "interrogatories" and "discovery" (or their foreign equivalents), than by seeking evidence specifically through the reciprocal consular procedure.

Thus while awkward situations arise in respect of the inter-

---

[53] 104 E.R. 725. 14 East, 582.
[54] *Bowling* v. *Cox* 1926 A.C. 751.
[55] The problem is further aggravated by the suggestion that the law of the place of the recipient is applicable. This is mentioned in Dicey, *Conflict of Laws* (8th ed.) at p. 156, but there is no English precedent, support being derived from the American Restatement s.354, K. 21.
[56] At p. 3.

national implications of a banker's duty of secrecy regarding his affairs, a jealously guarded obligation in so many countries, there is little general advice that can be offered. Obviously advice will be obtained from lawyers in both countries. Especially in relation to tax investigations English bankers have to remember that the authority given statutorily for information to be disclosed has to be interpreted carefully because an enactment or order taking away a right of privacy, making failure to disclose an offence, will be interpreted strictly. The obligation to disclose has to be express and not implied.

IV
Government Intervention

It is quite apparent that expropriation and exchange control are the consequences of Government intervention. Currency problems, including the ancillary subject of euro-dollars are also essentially dependent upon Government decisions.

EXPROPRIATION[1]

This aspect of law is in peace time perhaps the most controversial of all international legal problems. Essentially it epitomises the economic consequences of differing ideologies. It appears in several forms. There is expropriation by a Government treating all subjects alike. It may be with or without compensation. It may deal equally with foreign nationals in respect of property within the territory of the expropriating government or it may purport to affect property of its subjects or residents outside its own territory. The expropriation will generally be a form of nationalisation because there is usually no intention of re-distributing the assets; they are intended to become Government property. If expropriation is limited to a particular group of the community or to certain individuals only, it is normally described as confiscation. A little thought will show that similar economic results may be achieved by expropriating either the shares or the assets of a company, although in the latter case there should be a provision for payment of the company's debts. In a much broader sense similar economic deprivation may be achieved *vis-à-vis* foreign nationals by exchange control provisions, or, more simply, by punitive taxation. As we shall see, as the century has progressed the methods adopted have become more fair, or more subtle, according to the principles of the Governments concerned. Generally there is provision for at least nominal compensation; sometimes only a proportion, usually involving the taking of a controlling inter-

---

[1] The *Rumasa* case reported as *Williams and Humbert* v. *W & H Trade Marks* (Jersey) (1986) 83 L.G.Gaz 37, H.L. affirming [1985] 3 W.L.R. 501; stemming from the expropriation in Spain is to be differentiated because the expropriation was because the financial aspects of the organisation were regarded by the Spanish Government as unsatisfactory: See, finally, in the House of Lords [1986] 2 W.L.R. 24.

est. In fact one gets the impression that whilst 50 years ago the activating factor may have been a redistribution of wealth it is now an off-shoot of pristine nationalism.

The effects

Whatever its cause, we are concerned with its legal effects. It is to be emphasised that we are not directly concerned with the consequences in relation to *public* international law, that is the rules determining the relationships between states. It is true that the deprivation of the property of a subject without compensation is regarded by many international lawyers as a wrong giving the *government* whose nationals are concerned a right of redress. However the enforcement of a decision given in favour of a particular state is largely dependent upon the evaluation of the wisdom of reciprocity by the state responsible, against whom a decision by way of arbitration or an international court may have been given. Gone are the days of gun-boat diplomacy. No longer can the foreign secretary, like Palmerston, declare before Parliament,[2] like St. Paul, "*Civis Romanus Sum,*" knowing that the legal rights of a deprived British national abroad will be either restored or the subject of compensation. Even in the Western world the concept of prompt, adequate and effective compensation stipulated by Cordell Hull in 1939 is no longer regarded as sacrosanct, although the prospects of international trade have resulted in debt settlements, albeit on a small unsatisfactory basis, being effected with a number of Iron Curtain Countries.

It is in the sphere of *private* internationl law that we are concerned. What is to be the effect of seizure of assets abroad without compensation? Can they be claimed by assignees from the former owners if such assets come within jurisdiction of English courts? What difference does it make that the person suffering the expropriation was a British national? What is the effect of an expropriation that purports to assign to a foreign government assets situated in England? What is the position if the property was situated in a third country or the person suffering the expropriation was a national of a third country? Is the effect different if the expropriation has been achieved by the dissolution of a company registered abroad? Answers to most of these questions are necessary to assess the position of the English banker engaged in international business. There is first, however, the problem of the status of the "expropriating government."

Recognition of a foreign government

The significance of this subject is that frequently the first steps of a new government will be to acquire and control liquid resources. One

---

[2] This was on the occasion in 1850, when exorbitant compensation was extracted from Greece in respect (among other matters) of damage and ignominy suffered by a Don Pacifico, a Jew, resident in Athens, who was a British subject.

means is expropriation, often involving bankers. As a consequence there will be a practical question as to whether the expropriating government is recognised by the British Government. If it is not recognised, the acts of expropriation, with *or* without compensation, will have no legal effect here. Subsequent recognition may validate these acts.

There are two kinds of recognition made by the British Government and the Foreign Office are always willing to indicate the position obtaining at a particular time. In fact the evidence will be formally provided at the request of an English court. The first form of recognition is *de facto* and the second *de jure*. The former is when it is accepted that the new government is in control; the latter is when the new government is recognised as having established its legal title as a government.

The law in England

It is thought that a number of statements of the law may most clearly contain answers to the questions raised as to the legal consequences of expropriation. It is however to be stressed that, even in this country, a number of the answers reflect the elements of uncertainty and change existing at present in *public* international law. All public international law is not incorporated in the law of this country. Treaties and conventions have to be specifically enacted. However, it is often suggested that the part of public international law that is customary is automatically part of the law of England.[3] Thus in some measure the principles emerging from public international law will be an influence as to what is English law. It is also reasonable to enter a *caveat* regarding the statements set out below: largely because of the problem regarding the necessity of compensation, the true legal position both as public international law and private international law is at present much open to doubt. In particular this is so in the United Kingdom and in the United States.

The statements are:

(1) Except where otherwise specified, it is assumed that the government of the country has been recognised by the Crown as, at least, the *de facto* government.
(2) If land is expropriated it is evident that the local law applies whether or not compensation has been paid.
(3) If a chattel is expropriated then the same principle applies whether or not compensation has been obtained. Even if the chattel reaches England, as a result of a sale or otherwise, an

---

[3] *Vide* Dicey, *Conflict of Laws* (10th ed.) p. 1070 and Anton, *Private International Law* (as to the law of Scotland) (1967), at p. 2. To the contrary, see discussion in Wolff, *Private International Law* (18th ed.), at para. 13.

action brought by the deprived owner will fail. This may be seen from the leading case of *Luther* v. *Sagor*,[4] where all timber had been expropriated by the Russian government. It was sold and brought to England but the former owner failed when he claimed title to it in an English court. The position is the same even although the original taking has been by mob violence if a recognised Government subsequently validates the title.[5]

(4) If instead of a chattel a credit balance, a bill of exchange, an insurance policy or any other "chose in action" in the state abroad is expropriated, "delicate questions"[6] may arise as to where such choses in action are situated, although the general principles are established that a debt is payable where it is enforceable.[7] An insurance policy is normally regarded as situated at the company's head office,[8] although a bill of exchange is considered to be situated wherever it may be physically.[9] Theoretically, a bill of exchange embodies rights to a number of actions, but possession is usually a requirement.

(5) If any moveable item is "confiscated" in the sense that certain individuals or groups are deprived without compensation then the title will not be recognised here since the foreign legislation is "penal" or, on some views, because it is contrary to public policy.[10] However, with regard to land abroad, the failure of an English court to recognise any such confiscation would have little effect because of the obvious lack of control.

(6) Where a foreign decree or legislation *purports to have effect on assets outside* the territory of the Government concerned it will of course not be recognised in the English courts if it is confiscatory in the sense mentioned in (5). In addition however, it will not be recognised here if it is confiscatory in the sense that no compensation has been paid, even although the legislation may have been made with equal effect on all subjects of the Government concerned.[11]

(7) Where compensation of reasonable adequacy is promptly paid, the law is not so certain. It is submitted that the better view is that it will be recognised here in respect of assets situ-

---

[4] [1921] 3 K.B. 532.
[5] *Princess Olga Paley* v. *Weisz* [1929] 1 K.B. 718.
[6] *Vide* Dicey, *Conflict of Laws* (10th ed.) pp. 580–584.
[7] *Idem*, p. 883.4.
[8] *Idem*, p. 864.
[9] *Idem*, p. 569.
[10] *Novello & Co.* v. *Hinrichsen Edition Ltd.* [1951] Ch. 595.
[11] *A/S Tallina Laevauhisus* v. *Estonian State S.S. Line* (1947) 80 Ll. L. Rep. 99.

ated here. The point has been so decided,[12] but it is only fair to mention that the decision was perhaps prompted by the emotions of war-time and has since been the subject of judicial criticism. On the other hand where a Government has itself expropriated with reasonable compensation assets in which foreign residents and foreign nationals have been interested there is obvious difficulty on the principle of reciprocity in doing other than recognising similar legislation purporting to have extraterritorial effect.

(8) The most awkward aspect is where expropriation without payment is effected by the liquidation of a company set up abroad. Obtaining recognition of any title of the foreign liquidator may be an indirect means of expropriating without compensation. It is submitted that an English court will not give effect to confiscation or expropriation without compensation of assets in the English jurisdiction merely because it is achieved by liquidation of a company.[13]

(9) Where assets are situated in third countries the recognition by the government of that third country of the title of the new "owner" will not itself be enough if the authority of a person domiciled in the United Kingdom is also required. Although there is no authority it is unlikely that an English court would apply the law of the third country if, by doing so, they would be flouting principles that would bind an English court.

The banker's problems

Where the law is open to an element of uncertainty, as evidenced from the above examples, the application of an already complex body of law is more difficult still. Nevertheless, policies have to be formulated and decisions taken. Risks also have to be kept to a minimum. The circumstances in which English bankers will be concerned with the implications of such foreign decrees may be conveniently examined from a number of standpoints for which certain courses of action are tenable:

(1) The English banker will have credit balances or other assets such as securities that will be claimed by the expropriating party. Now the banker knows that in *certain events* there can be *no question* of the claimant's title being recognised. The decree or legislation may have been in respect of the property of particular parties or groups *only*; then it will not be recognised

---

[12] *Lorentzen* v. *Lydden Co. Ltd.* [1942] 2 K.B. 202, but as to requisitioning see *Bank voor Handel em Scheepvart* v. *Statford* [1953] 1 Q.B. 248.
[13] This doubt is mentioned in Dicey, *Conflict of Laws* (10th ed.), pp. 583, 584.

here. Again, although it may have been general in effect there may have been no arrangement for even a reasonable measure of compensation payable fairly promptly; also, there may be no specific attempt to endow the decree or legislation with any effect upon property situate outside the territory of the foreign country concerned. In each of these instances it is highly likely that an English court would refuse to recognise the foreign government's title. For this reason, it is appropriate for the English banker to ask for evidence of the decrees. If they fall foul of one of the requirements, as they so often will, then the banker can safely indicate that they do not appear prima facie to be likely to be upheld by an English court and that there can be no question of their being recognised until there is an English court order recognising the title.

(2) If the government abroad is a new or usurping government, enquiry should be made from the Foreign Office as to whether it is recognised as the *de facto* government of the territory. If it is not then the evidence submitted from the foreign government, so called, may be disregarded. If the asset is held on behalf of the foreign government or of one of its "arms" such as a Central Bank, it appears that recognition *de jure* is necessary.[14]

(3) If all the requirements appear to be forthcoming for recognition of the new title the next step is to suggest to any other parties claiming to the contrary that they may wish to seek an injunction to prevent your paying. This, if obtained, may not entirely eliminate any possible damage alleged as arising from your refusal to have recognised the new claimant forthwith; but from time of the injunction you are in a measure insulated from the consequences of continued defiance. Also for practical purposes your likelihood of having to face a claim against you will be much minimised by the comment, so often emerging from the court in such cases, that your requirement of formal confirmation by the court was justified. Any damage awarded against you is likely to be the smaller or perhaps only nominal.

(4) During this period of the court proceedings it proves very often in practice that if a balance belongs to a customer, whether a banker, commercial company or an individual, resident or domiciled in a *third country*, a compromise may well be reached internationally. This is likely to result in your receiving instructions from both the expropriating government and the former owner in common terms.

(5) It has to be remembered also that during this period the

---

[14] *Vide, Haile Selassie* v. *Cable and Wireless*, (No. 2) [1939] Ch. 182.

banker will be beset by demands from the party against whom the foreign legislation is aimed. That party will be anxious to lay hands on the balances and the assets in case the decision of the courts is against him. It may be true that he faces difficulty in every country, but it is common knowledge internationally that there is ample opportunity for assets and monies to be salted away beyond trace. There will be anxiety sometimes because it may only be a matter of time before the new government is recognised (at least *de facto*) with the consequential change of result.[15]

What should the banker do? His decision must contemplate, remotely, damages. On the other hand, there are a number of principles that may be invoked in his favour. Whilst a categorical statement of the law is not possible, it may be argued that there is an implied duty on the customer to insulate the banker from ambiguity and embarrassment. If by reason of extraneous circumstances the banker is placed in doubt as to the validity of the authority received from his customer he is not likely to be mulcted for damages if he defers his decision as to payment.[16] This can be established in some measure from the cases dealing with the position of a banker faced with third party claims or difficulties as to the title. It is, of course, true that until there is evidence to the contrary one recognises one's customers instructions in the face of all else. Yet, if the customer has been superseded, albeit involuntarily, a decree may be no different in form from a bankruptcy or insolvency arising in the jurisdiction of the customer's domicile; the bankruptcy may have come about in circumstances where such loss of control of assets would not have resulted in similar circumstances in the United Kingdom.

(6) The banker will be affected by practical circumstances. What are the damages against him in each alternative case? For example he will incline to pay an irrevocable documentary credit, where perishables are involved, despite a suggestion that the beneficiary's right has been expropriated by, say, a government body on whose behalf the documents are presented. Where however the consequences of taking the wrong view appear to mean nothing more than the inability of the beneficiary to withdraw money into his own control, the potential damage will appear to be smaller and the banker may decide to take no action, pending clarification.

(7) Again a practical line is to cast around for a good indemnity. This surpasses all the legal theory in the world. Sometimes a

---

[15] This happened in the case of *Banco de Bilbao* v. *Sancha* [1938] 2 K.B. 176.
[16] This receives some support from *Banque Belge pour l'Etranger* v. *Hambrouck* [1921] 1 K.B. 321.

banking or commercial institution of repute will be willing to provide such cover for its associate.

Summary

It will have been evident from the foregoing that the subject of expropriation is one in which the law is more deeply surrounded by doubt than in any other sphere that we have considered. It is axiomatic that the practical consequence to which we referred in general terms in the first chapter is that a view has to be taken more often than with matters about which the law is less controversial. In making such assessment the maximum information as to the probable legal position is of obvious importance. As to the rest the judgment and ingenuity of the banker will usually suffice. The major factors may be summarised as follows:

(1) Where there is no compensation payable reasonably promptly *or* where there has been the taking of property from particular individuals or groups, *or* where there is no British recognition of the foreign government *or* where the expropriation does not purport to have effect outside the territory of the foreign government, the expropriation of assets in England, or of assets controlled from England should be disregarded for the time being.

(2) While any of the points in (1) above obtain the banker should not experience difficulty with the party claiming to be the new owner.

(3) If the evidence is produced that none of the four above objections exists it may frequently be prudent to give those maintaining that the new claimants have no title an opportunity to obtain an injunction.

(4) A banker may pay over or hand over to the court but this will not always save him from damages if he had clear evidence of the valid title of one or the other contenders.

(5) Often the opposing parties will compromise, which compromise the English banker should ensure incorporates the settlement of the breach of contract claims against him that no doubt both contenders may purport to have.

Perhaps the practical advice may savour "playing both sides against the middle," but it is not an unreasonably cautious attitude for a banker to adopt where the legal depths are to some extent unplumbed.

CURRENCY PROBLEMS

The basis of decision of legal problems relating to currency changed materially in 1976. The House of Lords decided that an English court could give a valid judgment in the currency of a foreign country.[17] At the same time, as a consequence section 72(4) of the Bills of Exchange Act 1882 was repealed (it dealt with bills in currency payable in the United Kingdom and provided for conversion at a rate of exchange for sight drafts obtaining at the place of payment on the due date). Section 57(2) dealing with the dishonour of a bill abroad was also amended to eliminate reference to re-exchange. Another consequence was the recognition of a garnishment of currency.[18]

The above decision also eliminated the arguments about the rate of conversion to sterling which eventuated sometimes to be unfair. In *Société des Hôtel Le Touquet* v. *Cummings*,[19] a British subject domiciled in England, had borrowed 18,000 French francs in 1914 from a French resident and in 1919 repaid in depreciated currency. It was held that he had discharged his debt.

However, the question of whether a foreign moratorium or revalorisation law, by which a debt is by law altered in value if currency has changed, is applicable will be ascertained by the law governing the contract as a whole. This is the law which the parties have indicated or are deemed to have intended the contract shall be governed, usually, in the absence of specific choice, the law with which the contract is regarded as having the closest connection. In *Anderson* v. *Equitable Life Assurance Society*[20] an American insurance company had issued a policy in 1887 in German marks subject to English law. It was held that the *obligation* being subject to English law, the widow was entitled to no more than the sterling equivalent at the rate as at 1922 when the policy matured and that, because the contract was governed by English law and not by German law, she could not have the benefit of the German revalorisation law that would have made the sterling amount receivable more realistic.

It is possible in English law to stipulate for a gold value clause tying an obligation to gold value, thus insulating against a change in rate.[21]

How a currency obligation may be satisfied

One may have currency in the form of notes and coin in a country other than in the place where it is legal tender. This may appear to

---

[17] *Miliangos* v. *George Frank (Textiles) Ltd.* [1976] A.C. 443.
[18] *Choice Investments Ltd.* v. *Jeromnimon and Midland Bank Ltd.* [1981] Q.B. 149.
[19] [1922] 1 K.B. 451.
[20] (1926) 134 L.T. 557.
[21] *Feist* v. *Societe Intercommunicale Belge de L'Électricité* (1934), A.C. 161. It is quite legal to make such a provision in the United Kingdom (See *British and French Trust Corporation* v. *New Brunswick Railway* (1939) A.C. 1, although if governed by American law it is void. Dicey, *Conflict of Laws* (10th ed.), p. 981. See also *Multiservice Bookbinding Ltd.* v. *Marden* [1979] Ch. 84 overruling *Treseder-Griffin* v. *Co-operative Insurance Society Ltd.* [1956] 2.

be a disturbing contention but it is submitted with diffidence that it is substantiated by case law. Whilst one can deal in London, Paris, Berlin in *rights* to dollars, the dollar bank draft, and the telegraphic transfer or cable is in fact a means of transferring dollars that form a balance in a New York bank, one cannot insist on delivering an American bank draft, however strong the bank, in satisfaction of an obligation to pay dollars in the absence of specific arrangement. No doubt in most cases, subject to any adjustment for interest, it will be accepted. Nevertheless the obligation to pay dollars can be satisfied in say London by the physical delivery of dollar notes. This is always, of course, subject to exchange control requirements, which are not relevant to the principle. It is true that a balance in a bank in New York is only a right to a balance of dollars, but it is an *obligation* that has to be discharged if so demanded in dollar notes, whereas in England a dollar obligation *can now be enforced* in dollars. There are two cases, that whilst not establishing the point go very far towards doing so. In *Pyrmont Ltd.* v. *Schott*[22] a loan, subject to the law of Gibraltar, of 500,000 Spanish pesetas, was held *not* to have been validly repaid by the tender in Gibraltar of peseta notes because the notes did not bear a "guia," the necessary authority for them to be legal tender in Spain. In the later case of *Marrache* v. *Ashton*[23] on somewhat similar facts it was held that the debt could be discharged in peseta notes because, although their import and export from Spain was illegal by Spanish law the notes circulating in Gibraltar were, by 1939, when the case arose, legal tender *in Spain*. This meant that the debtor could take the benefit of a very advantageous rate. These cases establish that by English law a contract may be *discharged by the provision anywhere of legal tender according to the law of the country by which the currency is issued*. Yet one cannot obtain specific performance. If one sues for a breach of an obligation to pay dollars one does not have to be satisfied by the sterling equivalent as at the date of the breach.

The consequences for the banker

Perhaps the most dominant factor for English bankers relating to currency problems is that the date on which the calculation is made is the date of the breach. If there is a change of rate between the date of the breach and the judgment there is accordingly fortuitous advantage to one or the other parties concerned. Thus it means covering the obligation by purchasing or selling the currency forward at the date of any breach of obligation to avoid risk.

Also, if one has a right to receive currency and there is a breach of contract, sterling, it seems, may be tendered, which could be of prac-

[22] [1939] A.C. 145.
[23] [1943] A.C. 311.

tical disadvantage to the recipient since the rate would be the rate on the day on which the obligation arose.

Again, if a banker is able to stipulate that English law is applicable, he is able to sue and obtain a judgment here despite a moratorium in the country of the currency concerned. In addition he is relieved from any increase that may be imposed by revalorisation laws. It seems also, that any provision introduced by the foreign country by which debts owed to English residents may be discharged by payment to a local currency controller also would have no effect on the banker concerned.[24]

Yet, if notes are circulating here that, in form, are legal tender abroad, they have to be accepted in satisfaction of a currency obligation, whether it be a commercial contract or a forward contract between banker and customer for the provision of foreign exchange.

It is of course possible to provide against changes in rate, on a gold value clause basis, but, except as between English residents who would normally contract in sterling, it may well be contrary to the national laws of the other party.

Yet one can stipulate for a contract to be subject only to the jurisdiction of English courts, but here again it is unlikely that such a stipulation will be acceptable.[24a]

A last point to note is to ensure, in relation to guarantees of customers' obligations, as well as the banker's own commitments, that there is a clear indication as to whether a reference to a currency is simply to relate to the currency in which the obligation is to be discharged or as to the measure of the obligation. That is to say whether it is simply to be the money of payment or whether it is also to be the money of account, *i.e.* of the obligation.[25]

Exchange control

Problems of exchange control are so closely associated with other currency problems as to be appropriately considered in that category. It is also a fact that many operators from many countries are willing to blithely pursue transactions that flout the exchange control laws of another country. They may have no assets within the jurisdiction and will personally be unlikely to be apprehended. Generally exchange control offences do not alone appear to be extraditable. This means that the extent to which there is enforcement, or even the recognition, by the courts of one country of the foreign exchange laws of another, may be the only sanction with which such

---

[24] In the case of *Re* claim by *Helbert Wagg & Co. Ltd.* [1956] Cho. 323, sterling payable to an English company by a contract subject to German law, was held by an English court to have been validly discharged by being paid to a German Government office in accordance with German statutory requirements.

[24a] See Article 17 Brussels Convention Civil Jurisdiction and Judgments Act 1982.

[25] This point was ventilated in the Court of Appeal in the case of *Woodhouse A.C. Israel Cocoa S.A.* v. *Nigerian Produce Marketing Co.,* [1972] A.C. 741.

adventurers are confronted. There is also probably nonchalance as to the extent to which a banker incidentally involved may be embarrassed by the illegality "thither" but not "hither."

Obviously this topic has a "will o' the wisp" element of uncertainty. Until 1945 the extent to which the exchange control laws of another country would be observed was the subject of conflicting decisions. On the one hand an obligation of an English company upon bills of exchange payable in London, was held as between immediate parties to have been discharged by virtue of the law of Chile by which export of foreign exchange had been made illegal and payment in pesos locally ordained as a quid pro quo.[26] On the other hand where an English bank opened an acceptance credit and the Hungarian customer on whose behalf it had been opened refused to reimburse the bankers concerned, the defence that to remit assets from Hungary was illegal by Hungarian exchange control law was regarded as insufficient.[27] It was evident that the legal position was either open to doubt or to a very fine distinction. Then in 1946 came the Bretton Woods Agreement, an international agreement among the nations participating in the International Monetary Fund. This was that:

> "Exchange contracts which involve the currency of any member and which are contrary to the exchange control regulations of any member maintained or imposed consistently with this agreement shall be unenforceable in the territories of any member."

This was incorporated in the law of the United Kingdom.[28] The first time that the new law came before the high authority in this country was in the case of *Kahler* v. *Midland Bank Ltd.*[29] in which case the final decision was given in the House of Lords. The facts of that case were that the Bohemian Discount Bank, a Czechoslovakian institution, had deposited with the Midland Bank in London Brazilian Traction Certificates belonging to their customer, Kahler. Subsequently they were claimed from the Midland Bank but the Bohemian Discount Bank (or their successors) refused to agree to their release although all parties agreed that Kahler was the owner. Delivery to Kahler, who incidentally was resident in the United States would have been a breach of Czechoslovakian Exchange Control Regulations and the decision was given in favour of the Midland

---

[26] *De Beeche* v. *South American Stores Ltd.* [1935] A.C. 148.
[27] *Kleinwort Sons & Co.* v. *Ungarische Baumwolle A.G.* (1939) 2 K.B. 678.
[28] *Bretton Woods Agreements O. in C.* (No. 36 of 1946). In *Mansouri* v. *Singh* (1984) 134 New L.J. 991, the purchase of air line tickets in a foreign country with a view to obtaining a refund in England was held to be an "exchange contract" for the purpose of the Bretton Woods Agreement.
[29] (1950) A.C. 24.

Bank, being basically in favour of the Czechoslovakian bank for whom the Midland were bailees. The decision caused controversy because originally Kahler had lost control of his shares through the exigency of the German occupying authorities, although, in the abstract, the case was one of exchange control law. In was held that there was no contractual relationship between Kahler and the Midland Bank and that he could not show that he was entitled to immediate possession of the certificates. He had to claim through the Czechoslovakian bank, and the court would not order that bank to act contrary to Czechoslovakian Exchange Control Regulations. The court did not have to rely upon the application of the Bretton Woods Act. However, the enactment was considered much more recently in the case of *Sharif* v. *Azad*[30] in which a breach of Pakistani Exchange Control had to be considered. Sharif, who was a Pakistani resident in England exchanged a cheque for 6,000 Rupees for Latif a visitor from Pakistan by giving him £300 in cash. The rupee cheque was drawn by Latif, the payee's name being left blank; it was however in breach of section 5 (1) (*e*) and (*f*) of the Pakistan Foreign Exchange Regulations Act 1947. Sharif took the rupee cheque to Azad, a travel agent who, after inserting the name of a relative as the payee, gave Sharif his own cheque instead for £300. This was drawn by Azad on his own bank but was postdated. When Azad discovered that the proceeds of the rupee cheque were being held on a blocked account he countermanded payment of his £300 cheque on which Sharif brought an action. It was held however that whilst the transaction between Sharif and Latif was contrary to Pakistan Exchange Control and *unenforceable* in England, the transaction between Sharif and Azad the defendant was unaffected by the Pakistan law because both were resident in England and it did not extend to them. Therefore the action on the £300 cheque succeeded.

Summary

By way of summary the essential factors for a banker to remember are:

(1) It is possible to satisfy a contract in a particular currency by payment of legal tender of that currency outside the territory of the country concerned and that, in the absence of *specific provision in the contract,* no other means of payment may be forced upon the creditor.

(2) That an English creditor may not have to take sterling since an English court will now give judgment in other currency. If he sues abroad the position may be different.

(3) By stipulating the application of English law the effect of

---

[30] [1967] 1 Q.B. 609.

foreign law excusing or deferring full payment is likely to be avoided.

(4) The date when money is first due and not paid determines the rate of exchange, so that to avoid possible loss as a result of a change in the rate before judgment it is necessary to cover forward as soon as there is a breach.

(5) Only when you are in a position to dictate the terms of a contract are you likely to be able to stipulate that a contract is to be decided only in an English court.

(6) An English court will not enforce a contract the performance of which is contrary to the exchange control regulations of another country. A third party cannot be sued here however on the ground that there has been a breach of such regulations.

Euro-dollars

I mentioned early in the first chapter that, except for documentary credits, as far as I an aware, the legal aspects of foreign banking have not been discussed elsewhere and that in consequence the problems had to be approached with diffidence. Especially is this so in relation to Euro-dollars. The only sources of assistance are the agreements that embody the various transactions. None of these has been litigated and the symposia held to discuss the subject generally do not appear to have adverted to the legal facets. In fact, on one occasion I enquired from the organisers of such a session and understood that they had not thought that there were any legal problems. However, I have seen one agreement comprising 20 foolscap pages and 8,000 words. It is by no means without its rivals for size and detail, and the smallest comprise some two to three pages. Thus we may conclude that quite a number of contingencies have been envisaged.

First, however, it is necessary to know just what is meant by Euro-dollar. They are dollars, or rights to dollars, which, if standing to the credit of a bank account in New York, are like other dollar accounts, withdrawable in legal tender, that is in dollar notes. Their distinguishing features may be best appreciated by looking at the reasons for their existence. These may perhaps have sprung primarily from the decline in 1957 of sterling as a means of financing transactions outside the scheduled territories. The need was supplied largely by the dollar. To avoid their own vulnerability that could arise from uncontrolled obligations abroad, many of the governments and central bankers in the borrowing countries imposed restrictions on foreign currency borrowing. Then the United States Government imposed on the lenders in the United States an Interest Equalization Tax so as to raise the cost to the borrower of dollars. While this discouraged borrowing from the United States by some foreigners the United States lender found his outlet in the non-resident Euro-dollar market. Lenders in the "market," wherein the *transactions are essentially borrowing and lending* were further encouraged by the impact of Regulation Q which limited the maximum interest rate that could be paid on deposits in New York. As a result American banks have large commitments by their London branches reflecting the extent to which deposits have been gathered for use in the Euro-dollar market. The lending and borrowing of these deposits represent the so-called "market." The element of competition is the interest rate. It is to be realised that there is a short term market, perhaps up to five years, and a long term capital or bond market for much longer periods. The longer term agreements are admittedly more detailed but much of their technical content is common to both.

The substance of the agreement

The essentials of a Euro-dollar agreement may be mentioned without pursuing variations. First, there is the amount of dollars; secondly the time that the borrowing is to commence, the facility sometimes being in the form of an option or a "stand-by" credit; thirdly, there is the interest rate, normally tied to the Euro-dollar rate of the London Inter-Bank market or some such equivalent definition; fourthly, there is the provision for continuance that is permitted within the total period of the facility, the arrangement being that, after appropriate notice given a few days before, say, six monthly periods elapse, the loan is continued at a new rate dependent upon the terms then obtaining in the market, an operation neatly described as "roll-over."

There are a number of other common features: as to a fee; as to the borrower bearing any tax that may be imposed on interest; as to a change to another Euro currency at the "roll-over" date; as to what shall comprise "default" *in addition* to failure to pay when due, extending to such matters as petitions, execution against the borrower or to the appointment of a receiver; the lender may, as with other loan agreements, require warranties as to the financial position of the borrower or insist that restrictions be placed upon borrowing and the giving of security to third parties.

The law governing the contract

There are, however, two aspects to which specific reference is merited from a legal standpoint. Most of the Euro-dollar agreements indicate that they are subject to the law of a particular country. Where the lender is a New York banker they are normally subject to the law of New York. Where the lender is English to English law and where, say, the lender is Belgian, to the law of Belgium. This, however, may have wider implications. It is probably true to say that, apart from dollar notes, one can only have dollars in New York. One can have also the right to call for legal tender dollars in New York. It is in fact usually expressed in a Euro-dollar agreement that the obligation to repay is by the crediting of a bank account in New York. Strictly, without such provision, an obligation could probably be satisfied, *in the absence of the consent* of the lender, only by offering legal tender. Normally this will be practicable only in New York. Invariably, in practice, the lender would take a telegraphic transfer credit or a bank draft. These comments are very artificial, but they are relevant when one considers what law is to apply. The law of the place of payment will normally control only matters relating to the *mode* of payment.

However the practical question is whether the stipulation that a Euro-dollar contract shall be governed by the law of the state of New York rather than English law will make any difference to the outcome, if in fact the place of payment in any event is in New York. It is submitted that there is such a difference. If, for example there was a moratorium relieving temporarily New York debtors or, to take an extreme case, there were to be a revalorisation of the dollar, halving or doubling the amount necessary for a debt to be discharged, then if the contract were to be governed by the law of New York and an action be brought in an English court, the creditor would be subject to the New York law. He would in the first example be unsuccessful and in the second, it is submitted, subject to the effect of the revalorisation. The justification follows from the case of the Helbert Wagg claim. There a German company owed sterling *payable in England to* an English company. A German law subsequently placed a duty on the German company to pay the amounts owing to English creditors to a German Government office. It was held, when an action was brought in England, that it was a good defence that the obligation had been discharged by the provisions of German law, since this was the law governing the contract. *This was despite the amount being payable in England*. On the other hand, if the contract is subject to English law, neither the New York, nor, in the *Helbert Wagg* Case, the German law would apply. Incidentally where English law applied to a contract and there was a Greek moratorium,[31] the place of payment being Athens or London at the option of a purchaser, the moratorium was held not to be applicable.

It is true that the Bretton Woods Agreement makes an "exchange contract," contrary to the exchange control regulations of one country, unenforceable in the courts of another, but a moratorium for all debtors would not be of the character of an exchange regulation. Neither, for that matter, would be a revalorisation law, which would apply to internal *and* external obligations alike. It is of course quite a different event from a devaluation.

---

[31] [1956] Ch. 323.

It is recognised that the two eventualities chosen are unlikely, but they illustrate the *type of* contingency that may arise since one cannot disguise that the so-called "market" exists by grace of the major central banks. It is one of the few truly free markets[32] perhaps being vitalised by the quasi-speculation of the customers and put in perspective by the arbitrage of the bankers. Changes that could affect Euro-dollar contracts are much less dramatic than the examples. They would however affect the obligation and are not merely exchange control laws.

Availability

The other point is more simple. It is that the rate is to be determined in the "inter-bank" market. If on one day, perhaps more likely in relation to a Euro-currency less common than the dollar, there was no market, is there an obligation to provide the loan if called for? If dollars can be provided, perhaps from a stand-by credit of the banker under a lending commitment, must he fulfil the obligation? Or, in the absence of a specific provision in the contract can he escape? With a specific provision there would be no doubt. Probably, the contract would be treated as frustrated. In this instance the effect would depend on the law governing the contract. So might, incidentally, the question of whether the contract was frustrated.

So far as English law is concerned, it is likely that the disappearance of the market altogether would be regarded as striking at the foundation of the contract in that it is to borrow and repay on the free Euro-dollar market.[33] If, however, there is no market just on the particular day only, the position may be more controversial. By implication it appears that the purpose of the contract is the acquisition from the Euro-dollar market and the availability is an implied term. There are arguments to the contrary,[34] but it is thought that they are less relevant. At all events this position is pertinent only when one party has a right to call for currency on a stand-by credit. If if were merely to be the "rolling over" or continuance of the debt already created the problem would have less serious consequence for the banker, since it would relate only to the terms of the interest. What does emerge is the commercial desirability of there being a standard form of contract or standard terms for inclusion. This may be difficult to achieve even to a limited extent for short term English based operations. Nevertheless, it is important if there is to be a market that the obligations are as near to common form as possible. This was recognised when the sterling certificate of deposit came into being. It was adopted by all, although much could be said and

---

[32] *National Bank of Greece* v. *Metliss* [1958] A.C. 509.
[33] See *Chitty on Contracts* (24th ed.), Chap. 25.
[34] *Idem*, para. 1267.

was said as to the merits of the "promissory note payable to order" as an alternative, it being a form known to the law of many countries for centuries past.

Summary

(1) Briefly, Euro-dollars may be noted as the creation of Governments through control of exchange and of interest rates.
(2) The essential is that the *transactions* are borrowing and lending, either immediately or at a future date. It is not a question of buying and selling.
(3) Many of the terms are now almost standard.
(4) Attention might be given to "the law governing the contract" and as to "availability" to see whether the intentions of the parties are fully recorded.
(5) Standard conditions, if evolved, would contribute to future equanimity.

CONCLUSION

If these chapters have provided solutions for any problems or caused thought on matters, that without such thought would have caused practical embarrassment, there is an excuse for having disturbed what may have been a partial oblivion. The cardinal principle, however, is that the lawyer must do more than warn. He must construct. The run of business, which one will be reminded has always worked, must not be overborne by complication. That, of course, does not justify failure to consider the merits of unobtrusive protection that it is open to the banker to achieve in so many instances.

Appendix A
Civil Jurisdiction and Judgments Act 1982

The effect of the Civil Jurisdiction and Judgments Act 1982 (given the Royal Assent on July 13, 1982) is intended to be the incorporation of the Brussels International Convention of 1968. At present so little of the statute is in force that it is more profitable for the student to know the promised achievement to be accomplished mainly by the incorporation of the Convention. This is that persons domiciled in a contracting state may be sued there whatever their nationality. (In this connection domicile has a very different meaning from that attributed to it by English law. Whether a person is domiciled in a contracting state will depend on the views taken by the courts of that state whereas at English law, domicile is almost equivalent to "permanent home"). In contract action may be brought in the place of performance or wherever the branch or agency concerned is situate. In relation to tort it is where the tort or delict is committed. Insolvency is excluded from the Convention mainly because it was anticipated that there would be an insolvency convention which has not as yet materialised. In addition to the above it is open to the parties to agree upon the court to which they are going to submit. This can be done as part of the agreement between them. If the subject matter of the dispute is insurance or an instalment sale there are special rules applicable.

It was announced of December 15, 1986 by the Lord Chancellors Department that the Treaty, which is appended to the Act will come into force on January 1, 1987. The Treaty was ratified by the United Kingdom on October 7, 1986. Without the statute the Treaty, although ratified would not have been part of the United Kingdom law. As it is the 13th Schedule provides specifically as to the coming into force of sections of the Act: otherwise it is provided that the Lord Chancellor may appoint by statutory instrument days for the sections of the Act to come into force which he has now done for the Convention as a whole as from January 1, 1987.

Appendix B
The Mareva Injunction

A most important factor in the administration of English law has obtruded in relation not only to international aspects but latterly in relation to the legal system as a whole. The matter is of international interest because it commenced in respect of foreign based dependents, if they were being sued in the United Kingdom, but it was thought that they may remove assets abroad in order to avoid the impact of judgment against them, the plaintiff could seek an injunction to prevent this happening if the defendants were subject to the jurisdiction apart from the Mareva proceedings[1] (the name comes from the case in which the point first arose[2]). It is essential that the plaintiff has a good arguable case and discloses all the possibly relevant facts.

However by section 37(3) of the Supreme Court Act 1981 the jurisdiction may be exercised whether or not the defendant is domiciled, resident or present in the United Kingdom. Thus the satisfaction of judgments from assets within the jurisdiction is available generally prior to judgment.

Notice of this form of injunction gives rise to obvious problems for bankers. The claims of the plaintiff are postponed to the priority of bank security, including a floating charge.[3] In *Z* v. *A-Z and AA-LL*[4] the law on this subject was specifically reviewed by Lord Denning, then Master of the Rolls.

---

[1] *The Siskina* [1979] A.C. 210.
[2] *Mareva Companies Naviera SA* v. *International Bulk Carriers SA* (1975) 2 Lloyds Rep. 509.
[3] *The Cretan Harmony* (1978) 1 Lloyds Rep. 397.
[4] [1982] 2 W.L.R. 288.

Index

Bailee and as Agent (Banker as),
   generally, 41 *et seq.*
   safe custody work, 42
Banker,
   concern with insolvency rather than fraud, 2
   interest in assets of customer, 3
   knowledge of the law, 1
   paying, 8
Banking,
   and the law, 1, 2
   as a profession, 1
   measure of risk, 2
   practice, 1
   primary functions, 7
Bankruptcy,
   insolvency abroad, 31
   priority against insolvency abroad, 31
   the need for speed, 31
Bonds,
   bail, 35
   generally, 35
   tender, 35
Bretton Woods Agreement, 56
   meaning of exchanging contract, 57

Characterization,
   a factor in a problem, 6
   an example, 6
Cheque,
   dual nature, 7
Civil Jurisdiction and Judgements Act 1982,
   commencement, 63
   internal application, 63
Cohn, Professor E. J., 4
Collecting banker,
   account payee cheque, 12
   as agent, 11–12
   as holder in due course, 11

Collecting banker—*cont.*
   consideration for negotiation as holder in due course, 11
   foreign bank as customer, 12
   measure of risk, 13
   responsibility to paying banker abroad, 13
Company,
   derelict, 29
   Russian bank case, 29
Conflict of law,
   application of foreign law, 5
   country with closest association, 8
   examples of application, 7
   nationality, 5
   Renvoi in practice, 6
Contractual capacity,
   of customer, 13
      corporation, 14
      non compos mentis, 14, 17
Currency,
   English judgement, 53
   garnishment, 10
   legal lender, 53
   problems, 52
Customer without title, 12
   banks stipulation as to engagement of agent, 12
Customers subsidiaries abroad, 36

Deposit banking,
   repayment on demand, 19
Discharge,
   of banker's credit balance, 30
Documentary credit,
   alternative view, 39
   ambiguity, 40
   applicable law, 11
   covering letter, 40
   precise language required, 40
   the indemnity, 38
   the Soproma case, 41

Doubtful debt,
    generally, 20
    security for what work, 20

English law,
    bankers problems regarding compensation, 50
Euro-dollars,
    applicable law, 59
    availability, 61
    fulfilment of obligation, 58
    Helbert Wagg case, 60
    market in borrowing and lending, 59
Exchange Control,
    of another country, 43

Forgery,
    upheld in U.K., 8
France, 10

Garnishee, 10
Government intervention,
    compensation, 45, 46
        effects, 46
        expropriation distinguished from confiscation, 45
        recognition of foreign government, 46
Guarantee,
    occasion of payment, 37
    where claims are made, 37

Infant customer,
    borrowing, 17
    with credit account, 16
Insolvency, 35 *et seq.*
    company dissolution, 26
    leaving England, 24
        and going to Eire, 24
    meaning of bankruptcy abroad, 35
    oversea company, 25, 26
    unregistered company, 26
    winding up abroad, 27
International banking,
    duty of legal advisors, 2
    resolution of problems, 3
    the risk, 2
Intervention of foreign banker, 19

Jurisdiction,
    E.E.C., 4

Jurisdiction—*cont.*
    submission implied, 5
    submission to a U.K. court, 4
    where a judgement may be enforced, 3
    where an action may be brought, 3
    the whereabouts of assets, 3

Lending banker, 18
    as unsecured creditor, 28

Mareva Injunction,
    assets abroad, 64
    general application, 64
    notice to banker, 64
    Supreme Court Act 1981, 64
Married women, 18
Mortgage, 7

Orders,
    Orders in Aid, 28
    proceedings abroad, 28

Paying banker,
    paying under advice, 9
    payment by agent, 9
    subject to law of country of branch, 9
    war time, 10
Place of incorporation,
    generally,
        determined by local government, 15
    of customers, 15
    ultra vires activity, 15
Prescription, 7
Private International Law. *See* Conflict of law.

Revalorisation, 53
    applicability of English law, 55
Risks abroad,
    appropriation, 34
    moratorium, 34
    payment on first demand, 35

Scotland,
    an equitable claim, 21
    insurance policy, 22
Secrecy, 43
    tax, 44

Securities,
    generally, 20
Security,
    realisation in U.K., 32
Set off, 30
Summaries,
    bankers problems, 49–56
    currency problems, 57–58
    expropriation, 47, 49, 52
    guarantees for customers, 38
    insolvency, 33
    primary banking functions, 22

Trustee in bankruptcy, 21

Undertakings,
    guarantees and indemnities, 33
        drafting of guarantee by banker, 36
        the counter indemnity from customer, 33
        relevant law, 35
    types of guarantee, 35
    on behalf of customers, 33